100 ANIMALS
THAT CAN F*CKING
END Y⬤U

MOOSE
P. 156

Voracious / Little, Brown and Company
Hachette Book Group
1290 Avenue of the Americas, New York, NY 10104
voraciousbooks.com

First Edition: July 2022

Voracious is an imprint of Little, Brown and Company, a division of Hachette Book Group, Inc. The Voracious name and logo are trademarks of Hachette Book Group, Inc.

The publisher is not responsible for websites (or their content) that are not owned by the publisher.

The Hachette Speakers Bureau provides a wide range of authors for speaking events. To find out more, go to hachettespeakersbureau.com or call (866) 376-6591.

Portraits of Mamadou Ndiaye by Butcher Billy.

Book design and production by Indelible Editions

INDELIBLE
EDITIONS

ISBN 978-0-316-45377-6

LCCN 2022931799

10 9 8 7 6 5 4 3 2 1

TC

Printed in Canada

CREDITS

Alamy.com: Animal Stock, 173; Auscape International Pty Ltd., 180; Daniel Poloha Underwater, 210; imageBROKER, 195; Jorge García / VWPics, 135; Nature Picture Library, 60; Steve Jones, 147; **Dreamstime.com:** Valentin Armianu, 54; **GettyImages.com:** Auscape, 42; Jami Tarris, 138; **Jonathan Martin/Northland College:** 183; **Mamadou Ndiaye:** 8, 9, 11; **Minden:** Sinclair Stammers, 88; **National Parks Service:** 23; **Shutterstock.com:** 2630ben, 52; AB Photographie, 215; Agami Photo Agency, 184; Aleksandr Ozerov, 222; Alex Stemmers, 173; Ali A Suliman, 45; Alta Oosthuizen, 149; Andrew Arestoff, 66; Andrew Balcombe, 141; Andrew Witcher, 112; Andrey Armyagov, 91; Angyalosi Beata, 82; Anton_Ivanov, 155; ANTON GUTMANN, 203; ArtMari, 41; Arun Sankaragal, 197; axell.rf, 94; Bangtalay, 42; Baurz1973, 108; bcampbell65, 68; Best dog photo, 187; Bidon People, 22; Black Creator, 24, 92; blue-sea.cz, 206; bmidgett, 221; bmphotographer, 87; Bobby Bradley, 15; Bodor Tivadar, 180; Bolkins, 19; Brazhyk, 19; Brian Upton, 193; bruna-nature, 174; CappaPhoto, 121; cd-design.co, 40; chamleunejai, 119; Chaos2Light Images, 54; Chase Dekker, 80; Chris Renshaw, 52; Chris M. Shields, 108; Christian Vinces, 101; Christoph Burgstedt, 162; Christos Georghiou, 83; chuyuss, 197; CK_Images, 127; Colombo Nicola, 31; Cormac Price, 34; Corrie Barnard, 190; Craig Dingle, 55; Creative Endeavors, 74; cvrestan, 127; Daniela Barreto, 59; Debby Wong, 35; DenisaPro, 219; DenisNata, 30; Dennis W Donohue, 217; dibrova, 44; Dirk M. de Boer, 174; Dirk Theron, 131; divedog, 81; Dmitry Kokh, 146; dptro, 113; Drakuliren, 167; Dustin Rhoades, 26; Ebrahim Lotfi, 91; Edgar Art, 110; Eneng Lindawati, 109; Eric Amoah, 46; Eric Isselee, 4, 51, 172; Erik Mandre, 123; Erni, 68; Eroshka, 133; Ewan Chesser, 145; Fazwick, 7; Featureflash Photo Agency, 204; Flat_Enot, 40; Frame Stock Footage, 222; frantic00, 173; FRAYN, 172; Funny Elf, 192; Gerald Robert Fischer, 150; gillmar, 185; Gonzalo Ocampos Lopez, 199; Grindstone Media Group, 48, 49; Gudkov Andrey, 129; Guillermo El Oso, 168; Gurkan Ozturk, 137; Harry Collins Photography, 177; hasky2, 73; Hein Myers Photography, 107; Hiko Photography, 94; Igillustrator, 18; Illusletra CR, 108; Imfoto, 159; In Art, 109; J.NATAYO, 200; Janusz Pienkowski, 158; Jared Cohn, 84; Jaromir Chalabala, 76; Jarrod Calati, 28; Jeannette Katzir Photog, 63; Johan Swanepoel, 148; John Carnemolla, 182; Joseph Agang ang, 44; Juan Camilo Diaz, 124; Jurgens Potgeiter, 220; jurra8, 219; Justin Tyler Barlow, 131; kamilpetran, 186; Karin Jaehne, 166; Kasira Suda, 6; Kate Macate, 93; Kateryna Kon, 90; kbibibi, 58; Kelly vanDellen, 157; Ken Griffiths, 5, 153; Kichigin, 207; Kim David, 206; Kristian Bell, 120; Kristina Vackova, 64; Ksenia Raykova, 79; Kyle Cr8on, 27; KYtan, 65; Lamyai, 50; Lemonade Serenade, 110; Leonard Stanton, 85; LeonardF, 140; Leonardo Mercon, 99; Light-Dew, 59; Little Things Abroad, 128; Luimi, 133; Lukas_Vejrik, 181; Maggy Meyer, 57; magnusdeepbelow, 151; Marcin Perkowski, 31; MarcosAmm, 98; Margas Vilbas Photography, 7; Mark Gittleman, 37; Martin Pelanek, 152; **(Credits continue p. 224.)**

MAMADOU NDIAYE

100 ANIMALS
THAT CAN F*CKING
END YOU

CROCODILE
P. 70

VORACIOUS

LITTLE, BROWN AND COMPANY
New York | Boston | London

CONTENTS

GOLDEN
POISON
DART FROG
P. 110

INLAND
TAIPAN
P. 120

BOMBARDIER BEETLE P. 92

BRAZILIAN
WANDERING
SPIDER
P. 152

(No, that's not
a dinosaur foot. But
did I mention that all
the animals shown
here are life-size?)
CASSOWARY
P. 54

INTRODUCTION

If you've picked up this book, you're probably wondering how I ended up ruining ducks and otters for a living. So here's my character arc: In 2020, I was working as an environmental field technician when the pandemic hit. The day before I was laid off, I downloaded TikTok and started posting comedic skits out of boredom. On June 13, I posted my first animal-related video about a giant moose (have you seen what they look like next to a car??). Two weeks later, I had gained 100,000 followers, mostly on the heels of a video about prehistoric animals that "make me seriously question God" (actual quote, by the way).

I knew I was on to something, and, after a few more weeks of traumatizing and educating people with random facts about the animal kingdom, that number rose to 500,000. Since then, I've been posting nonstop about interesting, weird, questionable, and downright disturbing aspects of the animal kingdom, all while making people laugh (and likely sending a good number to counseling). A little over a year after that first video about the antlered Grim Reaper that is the moose, I had 10 million followers on TikTok, which I still can't even wrap my head around.

People often ask where my interest in animals came from, and honestly, there is no one answer. So here are eight reasons why I am the way I am.

1   *Zoo Books* (left)—you nineties kids might remember the commercials. I had them all and, fun fact, the elephant, or what I consider the most perfect animal, is the first book I ever received. Go figure.

2   *The Most Extreme* show was basically my bible because I watched it religiously. I wasn't allowed to watch TV on weekdays, but since the documentary series was technically educational, I could get away with it. If you watch this show and watch my videos, you can definitely see the influence.

3 *Zoo Tycoon 2* was my first video game. Basically, you just build a zoo and, for some reason, five-year-old me couldn't get enough of it. Also, I used to set the lions free and then watch them merk the guests. So yeah, I might have been a psychopath at one point.

4 I think I was like seven when I fell for *The Complete Book of Animals*. I had like hundreds of animal books but for some reason this one was my favorite. I actually lost it for like a year and a half in somebody's house in another state and my seven-year-old mind did not know peace until I got it back.

5 I had a talking toy that tells you facts about endangered species. I recently pulled it out and it still works.

6 *Zoo Vet* was also one of my favorite games. I would honestly spend hours playing it. I couldn't tell my left from right but I could tell you how to check for tuberculosis in the camel or how to treat diarrhea in a chimp.

7 Steve Irwin, but if you've watched my videos, you already know that.

8 *National Geographic for Kids* magazine, which I would get every month.

But honestly, I really don't know. I didn't like animals because I had all those things—I had all those things because I already liked animals. I don't know where it came from. I would make these little books full of animal drawings when I was three years old, and I have no idea what made me do it. I think I was just a weird-ass kid, and some things just don't change.

This book is filled with all kinds of interesting animals that can all activate your life insurance and put an RIP in front of your name. I've given them each a merk rating on a scale of 1–10, which takes into account an animal's tendency to aggression; how it interacts with other animals; how many fatal encounters with humans occur a year; how easily one could kill a human; and toxicity. But mostly it is my own admittedly biased opinion.

When I was little,
I went to the Bronx Zoo.
When I came back home,
I told my mom I wanted
to be a zookeeper
when I grew up.

100 ANIMALS THAT CAN

AFRICAN CRESTED PORC
AFRICAN WILD DOG AMERIC
TAILED DEER AUSTRA
HORNET BENGAL TIGER B
BLUE RING OCTOPUS BOX
GOOSE CANADI
CASSOWARY CHEETAH CHIM
SNAIL CROCODILE DOG DO
SEAL EMU FILARIAL
FUGU BLOWFISH GIANT AN
GILA MONSTER GIRAFFE
GORILLA GREAT WH
ANACONDA GRIZZLY BEAR
BADGER IRUKANDJI JELL
KOMODO DRAGON LEOPA
MANTIS SHRIMP MARABOU
MOSQUITO MOUNTAIN LION
PEREGRINE FALCON PITO
BEAR SEA SNAKE SECRETA
WHALE SPOTTED HYENA S
STONEFISH WILD BOAR WO

INE AFRICAN ELEPHANT
N BISON AMERICAN WHITE-
AN MAGPIE ASIAN GIANT
ACK MAMBA BLACK RHINO
ELLYFISH CAMEL CANADIAN
N LYNX CAPE BUFFALO
ANZEE COCONUT CRAB CONE
PHIN DONKEY ELEPHANT
WORM FRESHWATER SNAIL
EATER GIANT RIVER OTTER
LDEN POISON DART FROG
E SHARK **F*CKING** GREEN
ARPY EAGLE HIPPO HONEY
FISH JAGUAR KANGAROO
LEOPARD SEAL **END** LION
STORK MOREY EEL MOOSE
UTE SWAN ORCA OSTRICH
JI PLATYPUS **YOU** POLAR
Y BIRD SLOTH BEAR SPERM
ELLER SEA LION STINGRAY
WOLVERINE ZEBRA HUMAN

MAMADOU NDIAYE

AFRICAN CRESTED PORCUPINE

FOUND IN: SUB-SAHARAN AFRICA, NORTH AFRICA, ITALY

MERK RATING: 4

Do you know how much of a cheat code you'd need to have lions and hyenas afraid of you? The African crested porcupine has about 30,000 reasons to make predators not choose violence. If those foot-long quills get in your skin, they'll swell up and then push through your flesh until they hit something important.

A popular myth used to be that porcupines shoot their quills out as a form of self-defense. What they actually do is turn around and charge full force backward into a potential predator. Which is exactly how lions, hyenas, and even your pet dog can end up with a faceful of painful quills.

These rodents can injure lions so severely that their only option to survive is hunting humans. There have been documented cases of crippled and emaciated lions going after people and their cattle after being injured in an encounter with a porcupine. Which is why the same apex predators that can hunt walking tanks like the Cape buffalo will hesitate to go after a beaver with blades growing out of its back.

AFRICAN ELEPHANT

FOUND IN: AFRICA
MERK RATING: 10

Size does matter, and at 12,000 pounds and an average height of ten feet at the shoulder, no land animal is bigger than the African elephant. Squaring up with one of these is canceling your subscription to living. And they're about it, too: Some of the largest land mammals on the planet, like hippos and rhinoceroses, can get knocked over like a bowling pin by a motivated adult elephant. And with a pair of tusks, they can easily one-shot any opponent foolish enough to try them.

Also, there's nothing else like them. Bears, cats, and dogs look somewhat alike. Nothing on this planet looks like a big, overgrown, walking tank with tusks and a ridiculously long nose. Speaking of which, that trunk has 40,000 muscles and can lift 700 pounds. This pachyderm has more muscles in its nose than in your entire family tree combined.

But best of all, African elephants are smart. They're intelligent enough to remember for years (probably decades), learn to use tools, solve problems, and they even have empathy. They've been known to value human lives enough to save them. In 2012, after Lawrence Anthony, dubbed "The Elephant Whisperer," passed away, a herd of elephants traveled for miles to his home, in an almost eerie funeral-like procession. While the myth that elephants see humans as cute isn't true, that apparently doesn't stop them from seeing (some of) us as family.

At the end of the day, African elephants are one of the most intelligent, unique, and complex animals in the world. But with a tanky build, a trunk that can powerlift hundreds of pounds, and a devious mind, they can also be the world's most dangerous (when they want to be).

MAMADOU NDIAYE

Elephants are such powerhouses that they can even take lives accidentally. In India, a herd of elephants got drunk off fermented fruit and, during their inebriated antics, destroyed sixty homes and merked three people.

SURVIVING AN ELEPHANT

Notice I said "elephant" and not "elephant attack." That's because if an elephant decides it wants to hurt you, there isn't a force in nature that's gonna save you. Forget being sent to Jesus—a pissed-off elephant will send your soul straight to oblivion.

HERE ARE A FEW WAYS TO IMPROVE YOUR CHANCES:

- If an elephant approaches you and the ears are relaxed, it's likely a mock charge. If the ears are pinned back, it's gonna attack.

- Check out the trunk. A relaxed trunk means it doesn't consider you a threat yet. A curled trunk means there is malicious intent, and that elephant is preparing to end you.

- Stay downwind. Elephants have poor eyesight but a strong sense of smell.

- Find a barrier. You want to keep something between you and the elephant—a car, a tree, a mailbox—literally anything is better than facing this guy defenseless.

- Don't turn your back on them. Elephants take this as a sign of fear or submission. They will hunt you down and give you the world's worst face-lift.

- Distract the elephant. If it starts to approach you, throw a decoy object. You might be able to distract it long enough to escape.

IF THESE METHODS WORK AND YOU ACTUALLY SURVIVE, MAKE SURE YOU PLAY THE LOTTERY, BECAUSE YOU ARE ONE LUCKY MOTHERF*CKER.

If that doesn't work—scream. Loud noise might fool the elephant into thinking you're a possible threat and leave you alone.

" These homicide hounds can run you down at AS MUCH AS FORTY-FOUR MILES PER HOUR FOR THREE MILES. "

AFRICAN WILD DOGS

FOUND IN: SOUTHERN AFRICA
MERK RATING: 7.5

African wild dogs are one of the most ruthless stat padders in all of Africa. They are about the same size as the average pet dog but there's one terrifying fact about them: They never get tired. And there can be up to twenty of them on your ass. The punishment for resisting is they tear your guts and intestines out while you're still alive. (And yes, that is one of the worst ways to die.)

On a continent with vicious animals like lions, hyenas, and, worst of all, tourists, African wild dogs are the last thing you want to smoke with. They actually decide as a pack whether to go on a hunt, and they vote by sneezing. If enough wild dogs sneeze, they decide to hunt. This means that the difference between a zebra going home to its family or getting its guts scrambled could really come down to a wild dog with a pollen allergy.

PISSED OFF

Weird fact: Only the dominant male and female are allowed to lift their leg up to pee. The rest pee with all four on the ground. I don't know why this is a rule, but if a low-ranking dog pees with his leg up, he gets jumped, banished, and probably left to die.

Also, remember when I said they stat pad? They have one of the highest kill rates of any pack animal. Wolf packs have an estimated 14 percent hunting success rate, and lions flex at an average of 30 percent. But this African bush Cujo has an 80 percent rate, so if a pack presses you, there's an eight out of ten chance you're about to become one of the eight. Because they live in a dangerous environment, they're impossible to domesticate. Come at them with a rolled-up newspaper and you might just end up in one.

AMERICAN BISON

FOUND IN: WESTERN UNITED STATES AND CANADA
MERK RATING: 6

The great American bison provides an excellent case study of how even the most intelligent beings on the planet can be remarkably stupid. Because you would think weighing more than 2,000 pounds and standing six feet tall would be enough to make people social distance from you. But every so often, some idiot with a camera phone walks up to an adult bison for a photo op, only to go viral for getting steamrolled by this tank with legs.

Do not test a bison. As heavy as they are, they can run you down at over thirty miles per hour, meaning an animal in the same weight class as a car is also fast enough to snatch gold at the Olympics. Not to mention they can change directions in an instant and can even clear a six-foot fence in one leap. Oh, I almost forgot about their horns—and apparently I'm not the only one. Because every year, people get severely gored after violating this steroid cow's personal space. And the worst part is, 99 percent of these encounters are the human's fault.

American bison aren't naturally aggressive. They're not constantly looking for a fight like their distant cousins, the African buffalo. They're pacifist vegans that just mind their business and graze on grass. Unfortunately, they might be too well-mannered for their own good. It usually isn't until someone gets too close to one of their calves that people realize just what a pissed-off Appa can do. It's because of this misunderstanding

that in Yellowstone National Park, more people get sent to the hospital by this giant PED goat than by grizzly bears. The fact that we nearly hunted them into extinction must make it that much more cathartic when they turn a tourist into a Frisbee.

WARNING

MANY VISITORS HAVE BEEN GORED BY BUFFALO

BUFFALO CAN WEIGH 2000 POUNDS AND CAN SPRINT AT 30 MPH, THREE TIMES FASTER THAN YOU CAN RUN

THESE ANIMALS MAY APPEAR TAME BUT ARE WILD, UNPREDICTABLE, AND DANGEROUS

DO NOT APPROACH BUFFALO

AMERICAN WHITE-TAILED DEER

FOUND IN: UNITED STATES
EAST OF THE ROCKIES
MERK RATING: 9.5

The American white-tailed deer has to be the world's most average animal. Its presence alone probably isn't enough to be the highlight of your day. But at the same time, if you're in a car with friends, you're legally and morally obligated to acknowledge the existence of any deer on the side of the road with the phrase "Look, a deer!"

Deer are birthed in a vacuum of mediocrity and perish in a cloud of mundanity. There are about 30 million deer in the United States, each as unremarkable as the next. Don't get me wrong, I don't hate deer, they're not bad, they're just not great either. They kind of just exist, and that's okay. And that's what deer are—okay.

If you think deer are boring, your expectations are probably too high. When God storyboarded animals, he started with deer and went from there. I can think of about ten animals that are probably inspired by deer. And while a deer probably won't star in any movie unless you shoot its animated mother, we can all appreciate the simplicity of its presence.

Yet these basic animals somehow manage to kill 200 people a year on average in the United States alone. By running in front of cars, they wound countless more by causing 1.3 million car accidents. That's why these fluffy-tailed kamikazes are the most dangerous

DEER REVENGE

A deer hunter covered himself in urine and hoped that it would attract his prey—which worked, but not really. I'm guessing the buck wasn't thrilled about getting catfished by a pale, hairless primate in camos, and the man proceeded to get slap-boxed by Bambi. I don't know what month this was, but that deer woke up feeling Mayweather. The lesson here is that fades can come from barbers and pissed-off deer.

" Not only do they go after humans, but these

MURDER HORNETS WILL SLAUGHTER ENTIRE BEEHIVES AS WELL. **"**

ASIAN GIANT HORNET

FOUND IN: NORTHERN INDIA TO EAST ASIA, AND [NOW] VANCOUVER, CANADA AND NORTHWESTERN WASHINGTON STATE
MERK RATING: 3

Remember all of the headlines in 2020 about the coming of the murder hornets? These highly venomous Asian giant hornets erase about thirty to fifty names in Japan a year. In 2013 alone, they turned forty-two people in one Chinese province to the past tense. They apparently illegally entered the United States in 2019, with the first sightings happening in Blaine, Washington. One hornet nearly unsubscribed wildlife expert Coyote Peterson from life, so imagine getting pressed by an entire nest.

So why aren't they still front page news? Basically, the government said it was on sight. The Department of Agriculture made it clear that we couldn't give them a chance to establish in America. Hornet nests that were found were quickly put out of commission for the sake of our way of life. One nest allegedly had 200 queen hornets before they were all put in the pack.

That said, this homicidal vibe check is actually rarely ever lethal to people. Wildlife experts believe it would be impossible for them to become a permanent resident invasive species in America. So Asian hornets are like a TikTok trend or performative activism—a big deal in the moment, but they're overblown and they don't last that long.

ACTUAL SIZE

AUSTRALIAN MAGPIE

FOUND IN: AUSTRALIA
MERK RATING: 6.5

I think we all can agree that Australia is Satan's petting zoo. But do you want to know what animal there worries me the most? The magpie. This feathery, devil-eyed demon put legitimate fear in my heart because of two words: malicious intent.

Most animals in Australia will leave you alone if you respect their space. But magpies will seek out fades to run and smoke to give whether you deserve it or not. They're not typically aggressive but, during nesting season, they will turn up and choose violence every time.

These feathery spawns of Lucifer will dive-bomb and bird-smack people in an act of malice called "swooping." I had a friend tell me she wears a helmet during nesting season, an outcome of playing real-life Angry Birds. If you think I'm exaggerating, a magpie killed a baby in 2021 by swooping on her mom. One less person in the world because this hell canary decided to be a dick to mankind.

Did I mention they remember faces? Magpies can memorize faces for up to five years and will even teach their chicks who to trust, who to fear, and whose life to make a living hell. Piss off the magpie mafia and you've made a choice to live in fear. The best way to describe magpies? It's like if monkeys had wings, and no, it's not as cool as you think it would be.

" 'Magpie' probably stands for

MIGHT ACTUALLY GET PUT IN
INTENSIVE CARE **EXPEDITIOUSLY.** "

THREE ANIMALS THAT WOULD TAKE OVER IF WE WEREN'T HERE

CATS. They are nature's killing machine, but they're one of the few animals that ends lives for fun. These serial killers erase billions of animals every year. Without humans to check them, they stat pad and put entire populations on shirts.

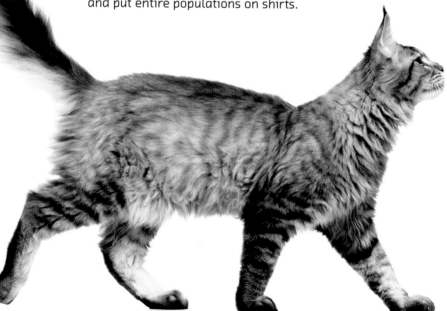

CROWS. Crows are smart enough to take over the world. They've low-key got Tokyo on lock. And because they can fly, these aerial assaults often go unpunished. As one of the most intelligent animals that can use tools, there's evidence that not only have they entered their own Stone Age, but crows also seem to be actively domesticating wolves in a way that sounds way too familiar. Combine their smarts with flight and remove humans and the world would get Hitchcocked.

GOATS. Believe it or not, goats are actually pretty OP. With their ridiculous climbing ability, they'd be able to reach food that their competition couldn't. But what would really make them a problem is how fast they multiply. In 1959, three goats escaped into the Galapagos. In fourteen years, there were 30,000, and by the 1990s, they had spawned 250,000 goats. It got so bad that we literally had to go to war against them.

BENGAL TIGER

FOUND IN: INDIA
MERK RATING: 10

Tigers are the biggest big cats, easily growing to about ten feet long and occasionally tipping the scales at well over 600 pounds. Yet for as massive as they are, tigers, especially Bengal tigers, are much more athletic than you'd imagine. They have a vertical leap of twelve feet and can reach forty miles per hour in short bursts. Their striped coat allows them to sneak up on prey and, in one explosive charge, ambush and kill them. Before their prey even has time to panic, the steroid Garfield will chomp life-canceling teeth through its windpipe. And with a bite force estimated to be 1,050 pounds per square inch, the jaws of a motivated tiger slam shut almost twice as hard as a lion's at 650.

As ambush hunters, tigers prefer to attack from behind. A common tactic used by people who live in close proximity with tigers is to wear a mask backward. The idea is that if a tiger sneaks up on you, seeing a face on the back of your head might discourage it from attacking. But since nature lives on veteran difficulty, tigers are starting to wise up to this trick. Meaning soon, the backward mask won't work.

As if that weren't bad enough, God's striped delete button has another terrifying talent. Tigers have been reported to imitate the calls of their prey in order to fool them into a false sense of security before turning them into a "was." Bengal tigers are said to mimic the mating calls of the sambar deer and Amur tigers can replicate the sounds of the Asiatic black bear. So now we have to wonder . . . how long until they figure out how to mimic us?

While tigers prey on everything from deer to cattle to wild boar, they are pretty picky about where they eat their meal. Which is why a full-grown tiger has been known to drag an adult cow for up to a quarter of a mile. They're even strong enough to lift them over a six-foot-high wall. No wonder people are terrified of these steroids with whiskers.

BLACK MAMBA

FOUND IN: SUB-SAHARAN AFRICA
MERK RATING: 8

The black mamba snake can strike you two to three times in the time it takes you to blink. They're also the fastest snakes in the world, able to move at thirteen miles per hour, which is pretty good for a guy with no legs.

If one bites you, you have about forty-five minutes to either seek medical attention or seek peace with your god because you're on your way. Not only can they season finale you in the span of a Netflix show, symptoms can occur in ten minutes and you can lose your ability to talk in twenty.

> **❝ They're the largest venomous snakes in the world, growing up to fourteen feet long, or**
>
> ## TWO AND A HALF KEVIN HARTS. ❞

Black mambas are the world's most dangerous introvert. They don't tolerate people within 130 feet of them, which is hella social distancing. And if you don't take the hint, they'll rapid-strike you like a machine gun. And like I said, if one bites you and you immediately turn on *Endgame*, you'll see your end before Tony Stark does.

BLACK RHINO

FOUND IN: NAMIBIA, COASTAL EAST AFRICA
MERK RATING: 7

Nature decided to give this freight train with legs a keratin horn and bipolar disorder, then it dumped this walking temper tantrum into Africa for plot development.

4 REASONS WHY THE BLACK RHINO IS SO DANGEROUS:

1. The rhinoceros is legally blind and can't see anything past 100 feet. Since there are no rhino optometrists, this emotional armor tank compensates by treating everything as a threat. This means they'll charge at butterflies with the same intensity as they would lions and hyenas.

2. And since rhinos can max out at 3,000 pounds, they prove that big people aren't always jolly.

3. As the second-largest land mammal in the world, a full-grown rhino really has no predators. Newborn rhinos might get targeted by lions but, since they're born weighing 100 pounds, they can easily put any human in the dirt.

4. When rhinos aren't putting their road rage on full display, they're actually really down bad. A male will seek out a female through her urine because you don't always need a rainbow to chase liquid gold. When he does find her, he'll follow her for days, hoping she acknowledges his existence.

The rhinoceros is definitely one of the more temperamental animals you'll see in Africa, but you can't blame them. Sharing an area code with lions, hyenas, and wild dogs would breed trust issues in any creature. Doing all that while barely being able to see is why having a short temper is actually the best defense mechanism, especially when you're built like a battle-tested unicorn (or technically, bicorn).

" Their front horn can grow to 24 inches long, enabling it to efficiently both

ERASE LIONS AND DOUBLE YOUR CAR INSURANCE."

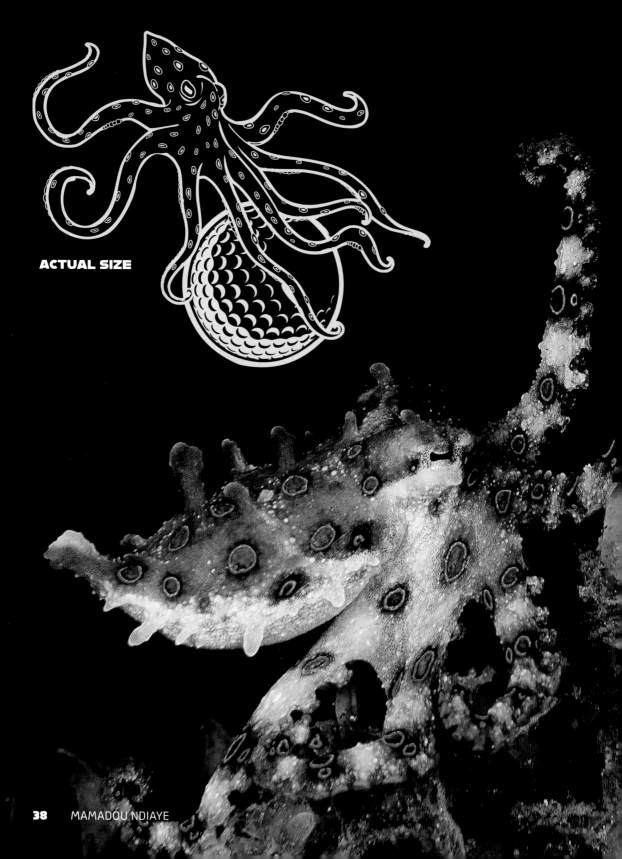

ACTUAL SIZE

MAMADOU NDIAYE

BLUE-RINGED OCTOPUS

FOUND IN: NAMIBIA, PACIFIC OCEAN
MERK RATING: 8.5

I had no idea the blue-ringed octopus is so small (the same size as a golf ball)—and somehow this makes the fact that it can erase twenty-six people with one venom-filled bite even worse. Most people don't even feel it when they get bit by one. It's not until they're paralyzed and have trouble breathing that they realize what happened. And getting paralyzed in the middle of the ocean . . . well, you can probably guess how that movie ends.

The blue-ringed octopus uses its bright colors as a warning to predators that they may be the size of a golf ball, but they're as toxic as they come. Unfortunately, some people see those rings as the opposite message and treat them as an invitation to pick up the tiny cephalopod. That's where it gets bad.

The blue-ring has a nasty little weapon, and it's a poison called tetrodotoxin, which is estimated to be a thousand times more powerful than cyanide. This potent neurotoxin inhibits nerve impulses, meaning the end game to being bit is either difficulty breathing or your heart just up and stops. One bite and you go from living fast to living in the past in less than half an hour. Just keep that in mind next time you see a video where someone calls it "cute."

SURVIVAL TIPS THAT CAN SAVE YOUR LIFE IN THE WATER

1
NEVER LISTEN TO HEAVY METAL IN THE OCEAN.

Not only will you attract headbangers and wall punchers, you will also attract sharks. The low-frequency vibrations remind the shark of struggling fish, and they'll come expecting food. And like the IRS, when they come expecting something, you're going to lose a lot.

2
IF A SHARK APPROACHES YOU, YOU NEED TO CALMLY CLIMB BACK INTO YOUR BOAT WITHOUT SPLASHING.

Sharks such as the tiger shark, lemon shark, and great white are elasmobranch fish, and they actually don't have legs, which means this apex predator won't be able to follow you into your boat because they lack the evolution points necessary.

3

NEVER HONK AT ANY ELEPHANT SEALS YOU SEE ON THE ROAD.

They'll see your car as a possible rival and will proceed to raise your car insurance with a testosterone-fueled blubber fit.

5

IF A WHALE ACCIDENTALLY SWALLOWS YOU, CURL INTO AS TIGHT A BALL AS POSSIBLE.

Because if it's a tooth whale, the sharp, cone-shaped teeth could tear you to shreds on the way out. Curling into a ball reduces your surface area and increases the likelihood of you surviving.

4

NEVER GO SWIMMING WITH A KANGAROO.

He's not trying to be your friend. Kangaroos will lead predators to water and then grab them and attempt to drown them—dudes to dingoes—and they will do this to you. Kangaroos are not afraid to get a life sentence if it means ending yours.

6

IF A CROC GRABS YOU, SHOVE YOUR ARM DOWN ITS THROAT.

It can activate its gag reflex and force it to release you.

One tip: Wear pantyhose in Australia—it might just save your life. The jellyfish's sting cells are triggered by chemicals on the skin, so if you're wearing pantyhose they can't sting you. Also, the pantyhose are too thick for the stingers to reach skin. So if you plan on swimming in Australia, putting on stockings might be the thing that keeps you alive.

BOX JELLYFISH

FOUND IN: COASTAL WATERS OFF NORTHERN AUSTRALIA

MERK RATING: 8

There are a lot of things in Australia that can put your face in a picture frame but the deadliest ones are in the ocean. Because in a continent surrounded by sharks, stingrays, and sea snakes, the worst thing you can encounter in the ocean is the box jellyfish.

This devil fish has up to sixty tentacles, and each tentacle has half a million sting cells that will fire harpoons into your body at the slightest touch.

> " Victims say the sting feels like being
>
> ## BRANDED WITH A HOT IRON
>
> and that's exactly what the scars look like. "

The worst thing about the box jellyfish is that for something that is the most venomous creature on Earth, you almost never see them coming. Most people don't even realize the jellyfish is there until they get mortally wounded. But by then, the countdown's already started. The venom is powerful enough to cause cardiac arrest in about the same time it takes to heat up ramen—only you'll be the one that ends up getting cooked.

CAMEL

FOUND IN: ASIA AND AFRICA
MERK RATING: 6

There's an animal you should fear more than moose. As deadly as that overgrown swamp donkey can be, camels are on another level. Nature gave them every possible way to put people on t-shirts and made it everyone else's problem. There are two flavors of this steroid llama: the dromedary, which has one hump, and the Bactrian, which nature somehow gave two.

Not nearly enough people know just how big they can get. The most prolic Bactrian can weigh more than 2,200 pounds and be over seven and a half feet . . . at the shoulder. If you accidentally rear-end a moose, you're probably losing your life, but at least the casket can be opened. You probably won't get an open casket if the cause of death is a camel.

Because even though camels eat grass and grains, nature gave them a meat-eater's mouthpiece as a sick joke. Canine teeth help them crush woody plants, but they also mean that if a camel bites you, that's a part you are not getting back. Also, you'll hate me for saying it, but they have flesh teeth. Their mouth is covered in papillae that help them force food down their throat. Technically not harmful, but this is what their mouth looks like.

Beyond their size, camels can run you down at forty miles per hour, which I don't think they get enough credit for. Plus their sharp toenails that protect them from hot shifting sand can also shatter your rib cage with one kick. Also, they can swim, and they're very good at it. Kharai camels are a type of dromedary that can quite literally pull up on you in the ocean. All this proves that whoever designed camels was fresh out of fucks to give.

OU NDIAYE

One man in India accidentally left his camel tied up outside during a heat wave, and he rushed to go untie it. To get revenge, the camel suplexed him, then decapitated him by chewing on his neck until his head and body were divorced.

CANADA GOOSE

FOUND IN: NORTH AMERICA AND SOMETIMES NORTHERN EUROPE
MERK RATING: 3 (BUT THEIR ATTITUDE MATCHES A 10)

Why are geese the Karens of the bird world? Well, male geese are more aggressive, so they're more likely to be the ones who try to throw hands. They're territorial and extremely protective of their families, and they'll attack anything that poses a threat. Geese nests are usually well hidden, so half the time you don't even realize you're walking in a danger zone.

Geese usually warn you by standing up and unfurling their wings, in what I like to call the "Come at me, bro." Ignore these signs, and that's when things get ugly. If a goose decides to attack you, don't turn your back on it. They have no morals and they will hit you from behind. Plus, they can sense fear. (There's no scientific evidence to back up that claim; I'm speaking strictly from personal experience.)

Since geese, especially Canada geese, are around humans so often, not only are they not afraid of us, they don't respect us. They don't give a sh . . . actually, they do—up to ninety-two times a day. Goose poop can destroy ponds by causing an algae bloom, on top of everything else they do. These birds really are the worst.

" Attacks on humans have resulted in

BROKEN BONES AND HEAD TRAUMA,

mostly when people fall trying to get away. "

CANADIAN LYNX

FOUND IN: CANADA, ALASKA, MAINE, MONTANA, WASHINGTON, AND COLORADO
MERK RATING: 3.5

Let's talk about the devil's kitten known as the Canadian lynx. This cat looks like it would literally take you and your family out just for looking at it the wrong way. They typically prey on smaller animals such as moles, squirrels, rabbits, and small deer. They're great swimmers, agile climbers, and they have snowshoe-like paws that allow them to chase prey at over thirty miles per hour even in several feet of snow. This killer is basically Chuck Norris with whiskers.

Also, the lynx has sharp eyesight and really good hearing, making it an even better hunter. This cat could run all of North America if it was just a little bit bigger. Yeah, this is definitely one of those look-but-don't-touch animals.

If this Grim Reaper of the North wants you dead, dead you will be. Has a lynx ever attacked a human? No. Does that mean I want to give a lynx a chance to make me the first? Not really. I've seen some people have lynx as pets, which I just don't get. Look this cat in the eyes and tell me this doesn't look like the type of animal that would merk you in your sleep just because it decides it doesn't like you anymore. These wildcats have been known to take down caribou, so what would make you think they care about you?

ANIMALS THAT LOOK DEADLY BUT AREN'T, PART 1

A **WHIP SCORPION** looks like it crawled out of a Stephen King wet dream, but they don't bite and they don't produce venom. Even though they look like aliens, they're actually massive pushovers. They're perfectly harmless, and the only damage they can do is reduce the property value of your house.

The **BLACK WIDOW** doesn't exactly have the best reputation. And the spider's not popular either. While they look terrifying, they rarely bite. Studies show that even after getting poked several times, a spider still won't attack. And when they do, their bites are rarely fatal.

PIRANHA got hoed by the media, but they're virtually zero threat to people. They're scavengers, meaning if they're eating something, it's probably already dead. Attacks are extremely rare. Most of the time you could literally be sitting in the middle of a feeding frenzy and not get touched.

The **MILK SNAKE** (below) may look like it can end you, but it is 100 percent harmless. When threatened, it would much rather slither away. They only look dangerous because they wear the same gang colors as the coral snake (inset, below right), which actually will put you on a t-shirt.

CAPE BUFFALO

FOUND IN: AFRICA AND SOUTHEAST ASIA
MERK RATING: 8.5

At up to 2,200 pounds with horns and an attitude problem, it's no surprise that the Cape buffalo causes at least 200 obituaries a year. With herd sizes of 400, if the buffalo bloods pull up on you, they'll stalk and circle you, giving you no other option than death. They're actually nicknamed "Black Death"—with all of the nonsense in Africa, they're the ones with that nickname. But they're so murderous, they have another: Widowmaker. Why? Cuz if your significant other goes out to hunt this beast in the morning, you might be single by the time you go to bed at night.

So how do you survive a Cape buffalo attack? You don't. If they can Mufasa a lion, then what advice can I possibly give to help you? "Make yourself look bigger"? "Stand your ground"? It's all going to end the same way—with your name in somebody's Twitter bio.

I didn't even mention the worst part. Even if you manage to shoot one, an injured Cape buffalo will retreat into dense, thick grass and wait for you. If you are mentally deficient enough to follow, the buffalo will ambush and gore you. Because this murder cow is also one of the most vengeful animals on the planet.

" Look at one the wrong way and you don't need statistics, facts, or Google to tell you that you're

FIFTY SHADES OF DECEASED. "

Are you still expecting advice on how to outwit one? Climb a tree. That's the best I can do for you. Climb a tree and pray the animal literally called Black Death doesn't have homicide on its mind. If they can make a lion do a barrel roll, they can easily make you six feet deeper.

CASSOWARY

FOUND IN: NEW GUINEA, INDONESIA, NORTHERN AUSTRALIA
MERK RATING: 7.5

I'm not afraid of birds, I'm just aware of them. Even if I were, I'm not talking about the backyard Tweety, wake-you-up-at-five-a.m. birds, I'm talking about this Jurassic bullshit with feathers. There are three types of cassowaries, and I approve of exactly none of them. This velociraptor-that-time-forgot can easily one-shot you with one swipe of his claws. Yes, I said claws.

7 REASONS CASSOWARIES SHOULD TERRIFY YOU

1 Out of all the ratites like ostriches and emus, cassowaries have the sharpest claws. That second nail is basically a dagger that can disembowel both people and dogs. By *can* I mean they have, they've done it.

2 They can run at up to thirty miles per hour, meaning they could chain-snatch Usain Bolt.

3 They can jump seven feet straight in the air, meaning this bush turkey could clear a Shaq.

4 They swim, so you couldn't Phelps your way out of meeting this one.

5 Female cassowaries are actually bigger than the males, and the biggest ones can grow to six and a half feet tall. This guy is six and a half feet tall.

6 The bastards kick. One man was taking pictures of one when the murder turkey proceeded to charge and knock him off a cliff.

7 I'd forgive all of that if they didn't sound like a Toyota on life support with indigestion. Seriously, YouTube it.

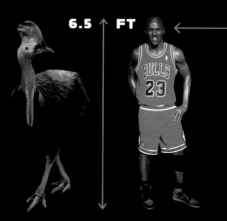

6.5 ↑ FT

" I don't even have a
fear of birds, I just don't want
MY THROAT SPLIT OPEN
by an overgrown homicidal
jungle goose. "

CHEETAH

FOUND IN: AFRICA, IRAN
MERK RATING: 5

Cheetahs are the biggest example of nature fumbling the ball. They're cats that are bad at being cats. Tigers have strength, lions have gang mentality, jaguars can do literally everything. But unless it's a 100-meter dash or a bird call contest, cheetahs take an L in everything else.

Cheetahs get bodied so hard they have trouble breeding in zoos, making them the only cat with erectile dysfunction. Also, cheetahs are so inbred that they're almost all identical, as a result of severe genetic bottleneck. The cheetah population was literally once so depleted that their only romantic option was their sister and, in some cases, their own mother. One myth about them is that their brains overheat when they're sprinting. But considering how their entire existence is already a roast, I wouldn't be surprised.

They're the only cat built to run and not run fades—their hunting success rate is 30 to 40 percent. They get pocket checked by lions and hyenas and, because they are lightweights, they can't even stand up for themselves. At least leopards can climb trees to avoid being bullied. But with nonretractable claws, cheetahs can't climb trees (or not that well, anyway). But what is retractable is their right to live— up to 90 percent of cheetah cubs get clapped before they hit puberty. That means the world literally gets an A+ in erasing cheetahs. And once again, if it wasn't for incest, they probably would be extinct.

But of course, wildcats are nature's perfect killing machines, and cheetahs may be the black sheep, but they're still part of that family. A motivated cheetah can still severely injure a human, especially once they go to their finishing move, which involves a crushing bite to the windpipe.

Cheetahs are so down bad their cubs have evolved to look like honey badgers so they are more intimidating. This African big cat has to impersonate a bush weasel just to have a chance at getting taken seriously. Wait, I forgot, you can't even call them big cats because they can't roar. Nature thought it would be funny to make them chirp like birds.

ANIMALS YOU DIDN'T KNOW COULD OUTRUN YOU

HIPPOS can write your death certificate and hand it to you at nearly thirty miles per hour. Nature gave them big bodies, stumpy legs, and malicious intent. The result is one of the cutest and most terrifying sprints Africa has to offer.

KOALAS can do the sprints at twenty miles per hour, even though they run like something nature didn't finish editing but posted anyway. Their running motion may seem like a video game glitch but they've been known to chase down ATVs.

CROCODILES can do the dash up to eleven miles per hour, but only for a short distance. If one does chase you, take that zigzag advice and throw it out the window. Not only does it not work, you're likely to slip and turn yourself into a headline.

WOMBATS are furry boulders that can cripple cars at speeds of twenty-five miles per hour. Meaning this athletic ball of fluff can get a ticket in the school zone. And when they apply pressure, you'll feel like you got hit by a bowling ball with ears.

CHIMPANZEE

FOUND IN: TROPICAL AFRICA
MERK RATING: 10

Genetically speaking, chimpanzees are our closest cousins and share more than 98 percent of our DNA. Their innate ability to manipulate objects and use them as tools, their complex social hierarchy, and their prowess at problem solving all point to them being one of the most intelligent nonhuman beings on the planet.

However, if nature proves anything, it's the smarter the animal, the bigger the menace (exhibit A: dolphins). And chimpanzees are one of the most homicidal menaces you'll find. Those complex social hierarchies I mentioned are borderline gang-like in execution. One of the most brutal things you can witness is what happens if a chimpanzee gets caught in rival territory. There are many accounts of a lone chimpanzee getting ambushed and attacked by an entire group, which can involve them tearing out its throat and genitals. In one case, a colony of chimpanzees rebelled against their leader, mauled him to pieces, and proceeded to EAT HIM. So, death by chimp is not a pretty way to go.

" There have even been cases of

CHIMPS IN UGANDA KIDNAPPING AND EATING HUMAN CHILDREN,

likely the same way they
do to baby monkeys. "

MAMADOU NDIAYE

or those of you that think of chimpanzees as just pacifist, fruit-loving vegetarians—nope. They're omnivores, meaning a good part of their diet comes from catching and killing other animals. Chimpanzees will make a meal out of squirrels and monkeys. In fact, they've been known to kidnap baby monkeys, bash in their skulls, and feed on their brains. Now what kind of depraved, savage beast would do such a thing? Well . . . us. Many anthropologists claim that early man regularly butchered children and removed their brains for nutrition. So when primatologist Jane Goodall witnessed a gang of chimps violate a red colobus monkey in a similar fashion, all it did was provide a mirror into the beta version of ourselves. Chimpanzees in Senegal have even been recorded hunting bush babies by sharpening sticks and using them as spears, eerily reminiscent of our own Stone Age.

It should also go without saying that no human on the planet is a match for a mature and motivated adult chimp. They're easily much stronger than any human and, with sharp canines and a crushing bite, they're capable of doing irreversible damage. But above all else, chimps are the best example of why wild animals always make terrible pets. As intelligent and human-like as they appear, chimpanzees are still walking assault weapons with thumbs. In 2009, a 200-pound adult chimp named Travis brutally mauled a friend of its owner and basically ripped her face off. No one is sure what provoked the attack, but some believe it was because the victim was holding its Tickle Me Elmo toy. But what Travis did wasn't a chimpanzee going crazy—the chimp only went chimp (points if you get the Chris Rock reference).

Few animals reflect the duality of nature better than the chimpanzee. It's fascinating to witness an animal with the cognitive ability, capacity for empathy, and similarity to man of the chimp. But they will also tear your arm off and beat you with it. And the most disturbing thing about them is that their viciousness is often a reflection of our own. Which is why chimps should be admired . . . from behind a Plexiglas wall

IN A PINCH

Those claws pinch with about 740 pounds of force, enabling them to break bird bones. Just for comparison, the bite force of a whole-ass lion is 650 pounds per square inch.

COCONUT CRAB

FOUND IN: INDIAN OCEAN
AND SOUTH PACIFIC OCEAN
MERK RATING: 3

If you value your mental health, do not read this entry—this is the only warning you're gonna get.

Meet your new nightmare, the coconut crab. This ain't Photoshop, this is real life. They're related to hermit crabs but everything about them is on PEDs. They can grow to more than three feet long from tip to tip and weigh nine pounds.

The biggest problem with this hellspawn with claws is they believe in the worst type of equality, meaning they eat everything without prejudice. Although these crabs eat fleshy fruits, nuts, and seeds, they'll also eat the carcasses of dead animals like cats and chickens. In fact, a group of these crabs made an entire pig's corpse disappear in only a week. Because they have the same diet as a garbage disposal, a lot of them are poisonous to eat.

And since nature is spiteful, they can climb trees. They've been known to scale tree branches and attack sleeping birds in their nests. Whoever thought that this crab was a good idea was on disrespectful timing.

These crabs are found on islands across the Indian Ocean and part of the Pacific Ocean. When Amelia Earhart crashed, a good number of people believe the reason her body was never found was that a group of these crabs turned her corpse into a cookout. And considering these crabs are scavengers that will eat literally anything dead, it's genuinely a possibility.

CONE SNAIL

FOUND IN: ANY WARM OCEAN
MERK RATING: 7.5

While the shell of a cone snail is pretty, don't pick it up, because it's actually one of the most venomous things on the planet. And don't think because it's a snail that it's slow—it's also one of the fastest things in the ocean. This murder slug can shoot you with a harpoon of venom instantly. Like getting struck by a pint-sized jet, this snail is able to hit you almost as fast as you can blink. That's not the only thing fast about them. They're nicknamed the "Cigarette Snail" because, according to urban legend, if you got hit by one you had enough time for a puff, pass before you puff, puff, pass away.

WARNING

DON'T BE *THAT* GUY

He's either a chalk outline or lucky to be alive.

These tiny terrors use their venom to paralyze unlucky prey. They'll put them to sleep with a toxin that's a thousand times more powerful than morphine, which works on fish and stupid people that pick them up.

If you are stung, you immediately experience extreme pain, swelling, numbness, and vomiting—but don't worry, it gets worse. The symptoms escalate to muscle paralysis, double vision, and difficulty breathing. And even though the cigarette story is an exaggeration, it could take only five to eight hours for them to connect you to God's Wi-Fi.

" They don't just use one toxin, though—
like Tyson they can have combos. They can have

FIFTY DIFFERENT TOXINS IN THEIR VENOM, WHICH IS WHY THERE'S NO ANTIDOTE.**"**

THREE ANIMALS WITH SURPRISINGLY HIGH BODY COUNTS

The **AFRICAN BLACKFOOT CAT** goes on some of the nastiest kill streaks you'll ever see. This tiny cat has a hunting success rate of 60 percent. They'll cap ten to fourteen rats or small birds a night. This death certificate with whiskers takes a life about every fifty minutes. In a world with cats like lions, tigers, and jaguars, this tiny bush cat is the most remorseless hunter of them all.

The **SHREW'S** ridiculous metabolism means it has to eat its weight in food every single day. This midget Bundy has to take another animal's life every two hours or else it starves to death. The most disrespectful kill streak of them all belongs to the African pygmy shrew, because it has to eat three times its body weight in food every single day. That would be like me eating 1,136 hamburgers in twenty-four hours. There's stat padding and then there's nuking the entire field.

The innocent-looking **SEAHORSE** is actually a carnivore that feeds mainly on shrimp. They hunt by standing still enough to pull their prey into a false sense of security before they snatch them up. This gives them a hunting success rate of 90 percent, which makes the little seahorse one of the most efficient predators in the entire ocean. If taking lives was a class, they'd be on the honor roll.

MAMADOU NDIAYE

CROCODILE

FOUND IN: TROPICAL REGIONS AROUND THE WORLD
MERK RATING: 10

In the not-so-distant past, there lived a bulletproof serial killer whose victims included everything from humans to hippos. Gustave was a Nile crocodile from Burundi. Scientists estimated that he was more than eighteen feet long and weighed well over 2,000 pounds. And with a bite force of 3,700 pounds, getting attacked by him was like getting assaulted by a sledgehammer with teeth.

Since Gustave was too big to survive on the usual victims of zebra and antelope, he instead put wildebeest and even hippos on t-shirts. He also likely resorted to cannibalism if he was ever low on groceries. And he didn't stop there, because this overgrown gecko allegedly had a body count of as many as 300 people. Gustave apparently would tear his victim to pieces and not even eat the mutilated corpse. Bro was a real-life stat padder, and the bastard was bulletproof, sporting three bullet scars on his body.

But the scariest thing about him is how he would go about taking your life. Like all crocodiles and alligators, Gustave slowly crept up on you in the water with only his eyes visible and the rest of his massive body hidden in the murky depths. And he would slam his jaws on you with the force of being hit by a car, strong enough to tear muscle and break bone.

If this bear trap with a personality attacks you, go for the eyes and the throat—it's probably your best shot.

With about sixty teeth buried into your flesh, 2,000-pound Gustave would have dragged you underwater and death-rolled you. How long you lived depended on where he latched on. If he managed to get a hold of your arm, he would effectively rip it right out of the socket. If he got your midsection, he would disembowel you, meaning if you didn't straight-up drown, you would bleed out. If you let him grab your neck, he would barrel-roll your head off.

Remember how I said he turned 300 people into hashtags? Considering how violently crocodiles kill their prey, it could be more—we just haven't found the bodies yet. Scientists spent months trying to capture him, but somehow a nearly twenty-foot assault weapon managed to avoid them every time. Gustave allegedly died in 2019 but we don't know how, why, or who did it, and we don't know how many lives he took with him.

Gustave is gone, but crocodiles are here to stay. They've been around for a good 200 million years with minimal character development. The whole "lie in wait and bite a zebra's head off when it least expects it" strategy works so well, why change? And why evolve physically when they already have eyes located near the tops of their heads, meaning they can get a good look at their next victim while being almost completely submerged. Now add the fact that Nile crocodiles have the strongest recorded bite of any animal today and sprinkle in the way they eviscerate their prey with the infamous death roll—when something works that well, don't mess with success.

DEATHSTALKER SCORPION

FOUND IN: DESERTS OF NORTH AFRICA AND THE MIDDLE EAST
MERK RATING: 8

With a name like "Deathstalker," it would've been a crime not to include this North African nightmare in the book. Scorpions in general are probably one of the most underrated killers, taking an average of 3,000 lives a year and injuring 1.5 million more with their sting. The venom that makes scorpions such a threat is normally used to incapacitate and paralyze their prey, but they're not afraid to use it for self-defense. While not normally fatal to humans, the venom becomes an issue when someone with preexisting medical conditions—like high blood pressure or allergies—accidentally meets the south side of a scorpion. In those situations, the neurotoxins can cause severe convulsions, difficulty breathing, cardiac arrest, and eventually a flatline.

Huge scorpions are not the problem; it's the smaller ones that you need to worry about. A good rule of thumb is that the larger a scorpion's claws, the less dangerous the venom. It's believed that the smaller scorpions are also more trigger happy with their venom and more likely to sting.

Which brings us to the Deathstalker, which at only one to three inches in length is considered one of the biggest scorpion menaces out there. Their venom contains paralyzing neurotoxins that with a relatively low lethal dose can permanently put you to sleep. If they get antivenom, healthy adults will usually survive an encounter. However, children and the elderly are at high risk to not recover from envenomation. No matter your age or health, getting stung is an unbearably painful experience. Size doesn't always matter, especially when you're packing poison in a small stinger.

MAMADOU NDIAYE

DOGS

FOUND IN: WHEREVER THERE ARE PEOPLE
MERK RATING: 7

Yeah, I'm not making a lot of fans with this one. Yes, dogs are God's gift to humanity, and we don't deserve them. They devote their entire lives to us and ask for nothing in return but our love and affection. I love dogs, and you should too. However. . .

Dogs kill thousands of people each year all around the world. These attacks aren't just beloved pets turning on their owners. There are also a good number of attacks from feral, rabies-riddled Rovers that pass on the infection to humans. In terms of sheer numbers, dogs are one of the top five most dangerous animals on the planet, with some sources claiming they take about 25,000 lives annually. Obviously this number is inflated by the number of dogs living in close proximity with people. But that doesn't change the fact that most dogs have the ability to put their owners in a newspaper.

That same predator drive that led us to team up with wolves still lives on in their domesticated counterparts. Did you know dogs enjoy squeaky toys because the sound reminds them of the noises of their dying, struggling prey? Thousands of years of character development doesn't just erase something like that. But really, this entry is more a reflection of humans than it is dogs. There are no "bad dogs," there are just bad dog owners. When a dog mauls someone, it's likely a result of this dog's upbringing and home training. Unfortunately, it's always the dog that pays the ultimate price.

Even the stereotypical "evil little dog" label is largely a result of human ineptitude. Many toy dog owners fail to discipline their dogs. Too often people let smaller, cuter dogs get away with things that would get pit bulls and rottweilers taken out of commission. Also, many see something like a chihuahua's small stature as an invitation to completely violate their boundaries and personal space. The result is an aggressive, angry little dog.

Dogs, in my 100 percent biased mind, are man's greatest companion. But let's not forget that they originated as an ancient apex predator that took down elk, bison, and occasionally the landlord of the North, the American moose. The sad part is, it often takes a headline in the newspaper to remind us what dogs are capable of. Still love them, though.

DOLPHIN

FOUND IN: IN THE WATER
MERK RATING: 6

Dolphins are a menace to life in general. First of all, they are racist. Dolphins will bully and harass other dolphins with different colorings and spots. They'll even assault porpoises by ramming into them and flipping them out of the water. They take it a step further by using echolocation to aim for the porpoise's vital organs like only a sociopath would.

They rape a lot. These water Weinsteins will form gangs of up to fourteen morally bankrupt males, isolate a female, and basically do what the Chiefs did to the Ravens the other day. Dolphins will also attempt to Kansas City Chief a human. Also, dolphins will grape-without-a-G underaged dolphins. Speaking of violating minors, dolphins will abort any babies they see just so they can mate with the mother and replace them.

Plus, they're straight-up sociopaths. They abuse puffer fish. They'll smack around a baby shark like a volleyball. They torture fish by driving them out to the shore, so they can just watch them suffocate. Dolphins also Shawshank each other just to assert dominance. I'm terrified of sharks, but you're more likely to get CSIed by Flipper than merked by Jaws. Just remember that.

MAMADOU NDIAYE

DONKEY

FOUND IN: ORIGINATED IN THE HORN OF AFRICA, DOMESTICATED WORLDWIDE
MERK RATING: 5.5

Donkeys are Black Air Force horses. If you're a rancher, you're better off trading your shotgun for a donkey, because you don't have to load a donkey.

Donkeys are naturally territorial and are *waaay* meaner than we give them credit for. Donkeys are aggressive enough to solo packs of wild dogs, which is why guard donkeys are way more common than you think. They're naturally sweet, but with their crushing bite and a crippling kick, they won't start the fire, but damn it, they'll bring the smoke. You won't just get your ass beat but the ass will beat it for you.

The reason donkeys are universally tougher than horses despite being smaller is because donkeys have a greater sense of self-preservation. Which is just a fancy way of saying the generational trauma of being hunted by bears and wolves, while also not being such pack animals as horses, has made donkeys more cautious, as well as more likely to kick in your chest. Obviously, a donkey can be a great companion once you've earned its trust (especially if you're an ogre with a Scottish accent). But break a donkey's trust, and expect it to do the same to a few of your bones.

" Not only will they delete a coyote,

THEY'VE BEEN KNOWN TO PLAY WITH ITS CORPSE LIKE A RAG DOLL."

ELEPHANT SEAL
(SOUTHERN)

FOUND IN: NORTHERN PACIFIC, CALIFORNIA TO ALASKA; SOUTHERN PACIFIC, NEW ZEALAND, ARGENTINA, SOUTH AFRICA
MERK RATING: 7

The elephant seal is the heavyweight champion of the Southern seas and the blubber-faced portrait of toxic masculinity. Male southern elephant seals can weigh in at over 8,000 pounds, and they use every bit of it when bulls fight for the right to their own harem of females. And with their deceptively nasty bite and a physique similar to a freight truck, these bouts can cause serious, bloody injuries. At the end, the biggest, toughest, meanest (and probably horniest) bull elephant seal earns the title of "Beachmaster," which comes with a harem of up to fifty lady seals.

Elephant seals are basically four-ton frat boys that care about only two things: food and another, less-PC f-word. This combination means that the male elephant seal can be six times heavier than the females he pursues. An amorous he-seal can not only crush his date in the process, but flatten any seal pups that make the mistake of getting in the beachmaster's way.

Elephant seals are such physical specimens that the only real threat to full-grown males are apex predators like great white sharks and killer whales, who see the seal as a one-man buffet. Other than that, these blubber bullies have the size and strength to make life difficult for everyone else, including people. Since elephant seals will never pass up a chance

=

to flex their dominance, you may leave your house for work in the morning, only to find this refrigerator with flippers hanging out right next to your car. So there's at least one person who had to explain to his boss how an elephant seal in his driveway made him late to work.

It's hard to envision just how massive these guys get. The largest land predator on Earth is the polar bear, and a bull elephant seal can be six to seven times heavier than polar bears are. It pays to keep your distance when you're on the beachmaster's territory.

They can be incredibly dangerous when riled, and those jaws could easily crack bone while tearing a chunk out of your arm. That is if they don't just body-slam you into oblivion.

EMU

FOUND IN: AUSTRALIA, NEW GUINEA
MERK RATING: 6 [POINTS FOR WINNING THE EMU WAR]

Emus are one of the weirdest birds on the planet. First of all, these bush chickens are way too powerful. They're six feet, 100 pounds that can outrun Tyreek Hill and jump seven feet straight in the air—like pick a flex, my G. Not to mention they have claws that could put a dingo next to Old Yeller. God was 100 percent laughing at us when he gave emus the green light.

Plus I gotta acknowledge the fact that the Australian military got memed by this thing. Two guys with machine guns thought they were gonna turn this flightless bird into a bunch of feathery packs, but instead they got demoralized by a rehab Big Bird. How do you go home to your wife and children after getting beat by an outback ostrich?

HERE'S HOW EMUS WERE ABLE TO DUB AN ENTIRE COUNTRY:

1   They're basically bulletproof. Their organs actually make up a small part of their body, which is why they are able to eat like fifty bullets. To the point where it took literally ten rounds just to take out one of these feathery tanks.

2   Emus are ridiculously, disrespectfully, unnaturally athletic. Not only can this Australian bush turkey sprint at thirty miles per hour, it can change directions like Messi. They were out here ankle-breaking men on trucks that couldn't keep up.

3 They're way smarter than we thought. Emus have lookouts in every flock. Having a leader that will stand guard and warn the others they saw soldiers approaching meant it was almost impossible to sneak up on them. They also purposely split up and scatter just to make it more difficult. Eventually, they started to recognize the sound of the soldiers' trucks approaching and would dip before they saw them.

4 There were just too many of them. Killing all of them would have put the economy in a pack. At one point there were 986 confirmed emu kills, but it took 9,860 rounds to do it. You can laugh, but we would have lost too.

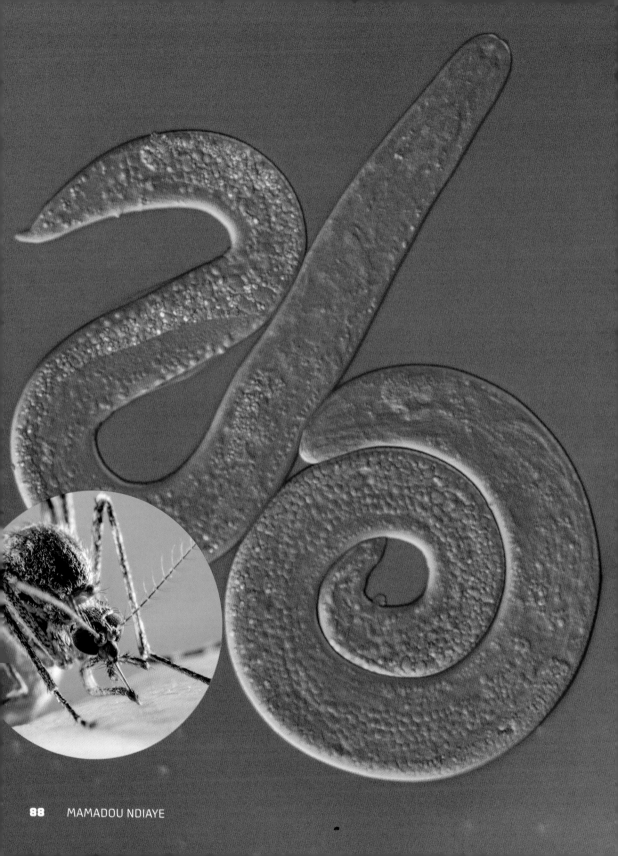

MAMADOU NDIAYE

FILARIAL WORMS

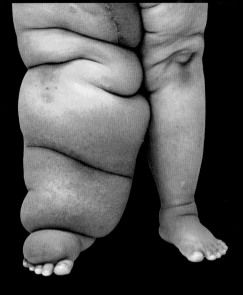

FOUND IN: SOUTHERN HEMISPHERE

MERK RATING: 7.5

When you think of a worm, you probably envision the slimy, writhing pink earthworms you find on the sidewalk after a storm. The truth is worms are by far the most underrated serial killers in nature, causing hundreds of thousands of obituaries each year while simultaneously infecting MILLIONS.

There are many types of these parasites, but I'm going to focus on the filarial variety aka roundworms. Because being invaded by filarial worms can lead to a disease known as elephantiasis, named after the fact that one of the symptoms includes your leg growing to about the same size (and sometimes color) of an adult elephant's. It all starts when your body is illegally entered by filarial worms, who gather in the lymph nodes. This blockage can cause fluid to build up in the lymphatic system, whose job is to help rid the body of waste. When these parasitic worms back up the lymph vessels and the fluid has nowhere to go, that is what leads to the nightmare swelling of the arms and legs that is the defining characteristic of elephantiasis. Of course, it's not just the arms and legs that can be infected. Let's just say your jock size might be an XXXL and you might have a hard time sitting.

The scariest thing is that you could be infected with filarial worms right now. For most people, they don't know until it's too late. All it takes is a seemingly innocuous bite from an infected mosquito to have your body become an Airbnb for nasty little parasites. And because these worms are as thin as sewing thread and no longer than your finger, you probably won't know they're there until you wake up with Dumbo-sized cankles.

FRESHWATER SNAIL

FOUND IN: ALL KINDS OF FRESHWATER BODIES WORLDWIDE
MERK RATING: 9

If you Google the most dangerous animals in the world, you find the usual suspects on the list—mosquitoes, snakes, dogs, and, of course, people. But there's one animal on there that you probably wouldn't expect to see.

" CAUSING 200,000 OBITUARIES EVERY YEAR,

the freshwater snail catches more bodies than an Instagram groupie in an NFL locker room. But why? "

Freshwater snails carry a parasitic disease I can't pronounce (schistosomiasis). But a doctor will pronounce you dead if they catch you with it. Affecting 250 million people in the world, these parasites will exit a snail, find you, penetrate you, and spend decades living inside your blood vessels. But it's the eggs that really do damage. They have sharp barbs and can get stuck inside you, causing symptoms ranging from anemia and fatigue to becoming a trending hashtag. All that from a freaking snail.

FOUR BUGS YOU SHOULD SOCIAL DISTANCE FROM

EXPLODING ANTS The Malaysian *Colobopsis saundersi* has the ability to nuke things with poison-filled glands on its body. This ant basically turns itself into a bomb and sacrifices itself by exploding. Colonies of these ants will go to war against each other. If one side looks like it's in a bad spot, then one of the soldier ants will self-destruct by bursting its glands, turning itself into past tense while covering its enemies in a sticky toxic glue that traps and destroys any ant it lands on. These ants will kamikaze themselves just to keep the others from getting ahead, like a true menace to society.

BOMBARDIER BEETLE Nothing will mess up your appetite more than a beetle's anal dragon breath to the tongue. The bombardier beetle's liquid "ass-salt" is actually a toxic chemical spray it uses to defend itself—kinda like built-in pepper spray but times a hundred. The chemical is created by mixing hydroquinone and hydrogen peroxide inside the beetle. You don't need a chemistry degree to know that will put almost any op on a milk carton. This chemical reaction is as hot as boiling water, which is what causes the beetle to release its butt acid like an Arby's regular. Even though that spray can RIP insects, the most it will do is mildly hurt you.

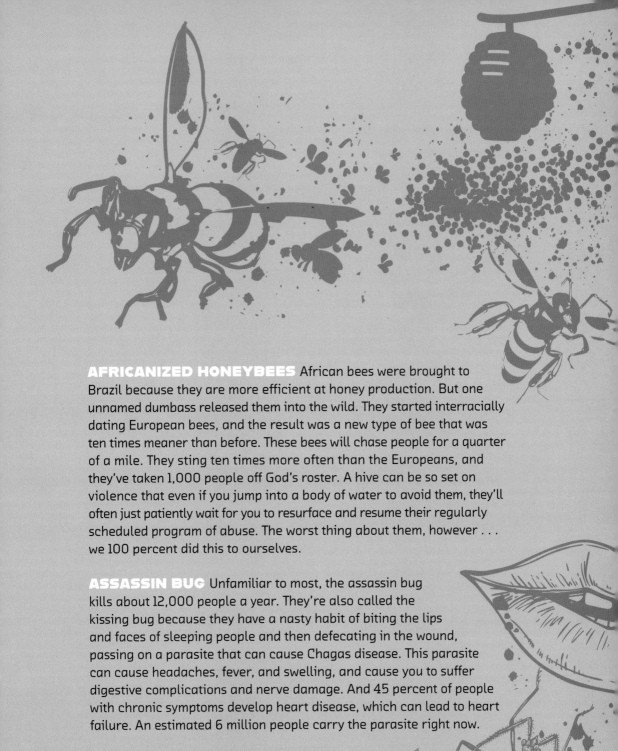

AFRICANIZED HONEYBEES African bees were brought to Brazil because they are more efficient at honey production. But one unnamed dumbass released them into the wild. They started interracially dating European bees, and the result was a new type of bee that was ten times meaner than before. These bees will chase people for a quarter of a mile. They sting ten times more often than the Europeans, and they've taken 1,000 people off God's roster. A hive can be so set on violence that even if you jump into a body of water to avoid them, they'll often just patiently wait for you to resurface and resume their regularly scheduled program of abuse. The worst thing about them, however . . . we 100 percent did this to ourselves.

ASSASSIN BUG Unfamiliar to most, the assassin bug kills about 12,000 people a year. They're also called the kissing bug because they have a nasty habit of biting the lips and faces of sleeping people and then defecating in the wound, passing on a parasite that can cause Chagas disease. This parasite can cause headaches, fever, and swelling, and cause you to suffer digestive complications and nerve damage. And 45 percent of people with chronic symptoms develop heart disease, which can lead to heart failure. An estimated 6 million people carry the parasite right now.

A fun fact—really a what-in-the-frozen-hell fact—people do eat blowfish. Considered a delicacy, it's actually safe to eat if you cut out the poisonous organs. But if the chef misses by even just a little, it's curtains. **The amount of poison it takes to put you in a newspaper could fit on the head of a pin.** Eating this murder guppy is Russian roulette, and every year somebody loses the gamble.

FUGU BLOWFISH

FOUND IN: NORTHWESTERN PACIFIC OCEAN
MERK RATING: 8.5

Arguably the most toxic animal in the world, on par with poison dart frogs, this tiny fish has poison 1,200 times worse than cyanide, enough to merk thirty people.

IF YOU WERE FOOLISH ENOUGH TO EAT ONE, HERE'S HOW YOU'D DIE:

- In the first ten minutes, you would feel tingling around your mouth and it would become numb, meaning you would start drooling.

- Then you would become nauseated, as your body desperately tries to get you to vomit out the toxic fish.

- Its poison, called tetrodotoxin, is a neurotoxin and messes with the nerve signals of the muscles, which is why you would slowly become paralyzed.

- After thirty to forty minutes, you wouldn't be able to talk, and you would suffer from dizziness and one hell of a headache. But don't worry, it gets worse.

- Once the poison reaches your respiratory system, you would have trouble breathing as the toxin shuts you down from the inside. (At this point don't bother praying, because whoever you're praying to is gonna see you very soon.)

- The lack of air in your lungs would put you to sleep. Since you wouldn't be able to breathe, there would be no iPhone alarm loud enough to wake you up. And all of this can happen in a few hours.

GIANT ANTEATER

FOUND IN: CENTRAL AND SOUTH AMERICA
MERK RATING: 7

Someone on Instagram asked me what animal is actually mean as hell but nobody realizes it. The first animal I thought of is the giant anteater, which can be more than seven feet long and weigh almost 100 pounds. We're talking about an animal that will straight-up swing on jaguars and sometimes win.

Giant anteaters have terrible vision, which is why they have something I like to call "rhinoceros syndrome." Because they're legally blind, they treat everything around them as a threat.

Do you want to know why scientists nickname it the "ant bear"? It's because anteater claws are good for digging up food and digging out graves. Anteaters eat ants and termites, and to get to them they'll break into ants' nests and termite mounds, which can be as strong as cement. They destroy the rock-solid mounds with only their claws.

Giant anteaters also have a secret weapon. Their long, bushy tail can be used as an umbrella when it gets too sunny or as a blanket when it gets too cold. But if you're a jaguar looking for takeout, that big fluffy tail can make it difficult to tell which end is the head. And guessing the wrong end is a good way to be left behind as a thing of the past, whether you're a jaguar or a human. That's right, this seven feet of steel wool has human bodies under its belt.

Giant anteaters pretty much walk on their knuckles so that their claws are as sharp as they need to be once they actually have to use them.

" If this murderous vacuum cleaner
EVEN DETECTS MOTION,
IT CHOOSES VIOLENCE. "

Giant anteaters have been known to severely maul zookeepers. In Brazil, a hunter once cornered a giant anteater. The beast proceeded to slash his thigh, severing his femoral artery and punching his ticket to the afterlife. (To be fair, it was a hunter; you roll the dice, sometimes you take an L.)

Anteaters are way meaner and more aggressive than you think. Even adorable tamanduas are a possible threat since they also have sharp Freddy Krueger fingernails. In fact, the T posing, which some might mistake for a hug, is actually one of the last warnings you get before things get rated R. Jaguars are one of the most feared animals in the Amazon, and even they will hesitate to test their luck against an armed feather duster.

At least the babies are cute. Watching them hitch a ride on their mother's back almost makes you forget that one day they'll grow up to become nearsighted assault weapons that could quite literally kill you.

GIANT RIVER OTTER

FOUND IN: AMAZON RIVER BASIN
MERK RATING: 6.5

There's an animal I personally believe not nearly enough people fear—and just for the record, it's not a honey badger. But it kind of is: Imagine if we took honey badgers, gave them swimming lessons, injected them with growth hormones, and, just to set the world in flames, taught them how to operate as a fully functional gang. So basically, we'd have 'roided up breast-stroking felony weasels with mob mentality and homicidal tendencies. But you don't have to imagine, because that animal actually exists.

If you haven't guessed it by now, I just gave you the police description of the South American giant river otter. I was not kidding about them being honey badgers on steroids—the largest ones can reach six feet in length. I'm only six feet when I'm lying and on Tinder.

But like with all criminals, to really understand this demon water weasel, you have to look at its family first. They belong to team *Mustelidae*, a family reunion that includes some of the most disrespectful things on four legs. I'm not going to bore you with a whole biology lesson, but the mustelid family you recognize, like wolverines, otters, badgers, and stoats, are all part of the carnivore suborder called *Caniformia*. And *Caniformia* are basically just dog-like carnivores, which include domestic dogs, wolves, coyotes, and foxes. But some mustelids don't have the intelligence of wolves and dogs, so they had to overcompensate by being nature's version of short-person syndrome, like honey badgers that will g-check a pride of lions right in their own hood; wolverines that will pick fights with higher weight class animals and still somehow not feel like the underdog; and which finally brings us to the otter.

For those of you that want to disregard this entire entry because you think they're cute, that's cool. Seriously, I completely understand— they said the same thing about Ted Bundy.

There are several flavors of otters found all over the world, but they all share one very important thing in common: They can swim, they're very good at it, and best believe they make it everyone's problem. Otters have a streamlined body, most have webbed feet, and both river and sea otters can hold their breath underwater for about eight minutes. But if swimming was the only thing that made these overgrown river weasels special, this wouldn't be an entry.

Giant river otters are 100 percent affiliated. Unlike basically the rest of their mustelid family, giant river otters are social and can roll up in gangs of up to twenty. We're talking about twenty vicious furry gang-bangers that each can be the length of a grown man. Using their numbers and teamwork, these waterproof wolverines will jump anything that ends up in their territory without a permission slip—and yes, that includes humans. River otters have been reported assaulting people for the simple crime of existing in the same lake or river as them. Serious otter attacks on humans might be rare, but it seems like at least once a year someone gets put on a headline after getting severely vibe tested by one.

" One woman was kayaking down a river in western Florida when she saw a river otter that she thought was adorable. AFTER IT LUNGED AND MAULED HER FACE, IT BECAME A LOT LESS CUTE. "

The most aggressive and homicidal of all the otters are the giant river otters of the Amazon but, granted, it's for a pretty good reason. They have to share an area code with top predators like the jaguar, the black caiman, and the anaconda. When your neighborhood looks like that, your only real option is war. Violence may not be the answer, but life is multiple choice.

And they'll use gang violence to intimidate much larger animals that would probably one-shot them if they were alone. If a jaguar can catch a river otter on its own, it's goodbye. But with the numbers advantage, the otter mafia can effectively drive off even the most motivated jaguar. This is especially true in the water, where they basically have a home-court advantage. Because in the water, river otters are much quicker and more agile than the bulky big cat, which is why an apex predator that literally claps caiman can end up getting humbled and straight-up humiliated by a hood of otters.

Speaking of the caiman, probably nobody's more of a victim than the smaller cousin of the crocodile. Because not only will a gang of otters jump a caiman and attack it from all sides, they often won't hesitate to eat the caiman alive. Remember how I said the stoat can take down prey ten times its size by exhausting it and biting the back of its head? That is exactly how giant otters can make a caiman's entire existence a living prostate exam. As cold-blooded reptiles, caimans run out of energy quickly. It's the reason crocodiles and alligators are ambush hunters, since they don't have the speed or endurance to run down their prey. So when otters maul the caiman from all angles like Rugrats from hell, it doesn't take long for the reptile to stop working—just call it a reptile dysfunction. Once the caiman finally gives up, the otters will put it out of its misery with a finishing blow to the caiman's weak point—the back of its head. Once the caiman becomes past tense, the otters will use razor-sharp jaws to tear the reptile apart and eat it.

Now if you feel bad for the caiman, know that giant otters will usually do this to defend their pups, since the game will snatch up any unaccompanied minors if they get the chance. But of course, they'll also harass a caiman just for wandering into the wrong side of the river wearing the wrong colors. They're basically the Crip weasels of the Amazon. They have no rules, no church, no morals, and absolutely no fucks to give.

GILA MONSTER

(IT'S PRONOUNCED "HEE-LA"—JUST WANTED TO GET THAT OUT OF THE WAY)

FOUND IN: SOUTHWESTERN UNITED STATES
MERK RATING: 3

This lizard is found in the Southwest, especially in Arizona. In the olden times (you know, before color TV), the Gila monster was thought to have a foul, bacteria-riddled bite that would drop a human due to infection. In actuality, they are armed with an incapacitating painful venom. When they bite, they'll actually chew to inject even more toxins into their victim. And by incapacitating, I mean it's widely believed to be the most crippling pain produced by the venom of any vertebrate.

But does this monster deserve its fearsome reputation? Not at all. Getting bit by a Gila isn't fun, but the chances are extremely low that it will be fatal to an adult human. Also, venom is physiologically expensive to make, and animals like Gilas and snakes avoid resorting to it. So if a Gila monster bites you, it means two things. Number one, it was a defensive response, and number two, you almost certainly did something to deserve it. Not only that, but because venom is such a

precious internal resource, Gila monsters often deliver dry bites. "Dry bites" means the Gila doesn't release venom but wants to send a message that it is not to be tested.

Add the facts that they're slow, sluggish, and typically nocturnal, the Gila monster is probably the "least dangerous" dangerous animal in the world. It takes so many things going wrong for a Gila monster to bite, let alone waste venom on a stupid human, that it would actually take talent to have it in your obituary. Unfortunately, its vicious reputation meant that, at the turn of the century, Gila monsters were often slaughtered by humans out of fear, proving that one of the most dangerous things you can be is ignorant. And that if an animal with the word "monster" in its name is afraid of us, there's a problem.

The Gila monster is one of the few venomous lizards in the world and the only one with an American area code.

Because a giraffe is usually the tallest thing on the dry open savannah, it's not uncommon for them to get clapped by lightning. When this happens, their heart basically beats itself to death.

GIRAFFE

FOUND IN: AFRICA
MERK RATING: 5

Giraffes aren't obvious killers, but here are some facts about them that slowly get more disturbing:

- **Males flirt by slamming their heads into the side of the female until she forcefully pees.** He'll taste test her pee to see if she's ovulating to decide whether to pursue her.

- Ninety percent of giraffe sex is between two males, and nothing is wrong with that—love who you love. But most of the time it's an older giraffe asserting his authority on a younger, weaker male. **This isn't an act of love; he's basically getting Shawshanked by a long-necked bully.**

- **Giraffes have hooves the size of dinner plates.** They've been seen on record decapitating lions with one kick, which is why baby giraffes hide under their mothers when predators attack.

- **Sometimes a mother friendly-fires her baby with a kick that shatters his neck.** Baby giraffes are just as likely to get accidentally killed by their mothers as they are by lions. Those vicious kicks can also be aimed at people if giraffes feel threatened.

Now, are giraffes these über-aggressive menaces to the savannah? Nah, we have hippos and Cape buffalo for that. But anything that can divorce a lion's skull from its body can't be taken lightly, especially when they literally come out of the womb as tall and as heavy as full-grown men.

THE SEVEN DEADLY SINS AS ANIMALS

ENVY is definitely the **common house sparrow**, because if she finds out her mate's been cheating on her, she'll proceed to butcher and abort the chicks he had with another female. Why y'all go after everyone but the actual cheater? I don't get it.

LUST is definitely the **antechinus**, because he won't stop spreading his seed until his immune system shuts down, his body disintegrates, and bro just becomes past tense. Dude experiences post-nut clarity in the afterlife.

GLUTTONY is the **Argentinian wide-mouthed frog** because it never stops eating. The only way this kamikaze Kermit stops is if it either chokes to death or literally tears its stomach open. This frog will die trying to swallow something physically bigger than itself.

WRATH is none other than the **hippo**, because every year they RSVP at least 500 people to heaven's house party in Africa alone. And let's be real, the number is probably higher, we just haven't found the bodies yet.

SLOTH is a **sloth** because that just makes sense.

PRIDE is a **peacock**, because being a show-off helps it bag a female, but it also helps it get bagged by a tiger. Those feathers make it harder for them to fly and impossible to see behind itself, which is why its biggest flex often gets it buried.

GREED is the **bowerbird**, because it will obsessively collect certain color objects to place in its elaborately built, massive bowers that it builds to attract the attention of a female.

GOLDEN POISON DART FROG

FOUND IN: COASTAL COLOMBIA
MERK RATING: 8

The poison dart frog is toxic enough to merk ten men. In fact, the amount of poison this frog would need to put you in a Twitter bio is about two micrograms. That means the lethal dose, as in the amount of poison you would not be able to come back from, fits on the head of a pin.

And the biggest frog op of all is the golden poison dart frog. I can't confirm that this is true, but allegedly it could put a full-grown elephant in the ground.

I give Australia a lot of shit, but we gotta talk about the nonsense that goes on in South America. You've got steroid Garfield-clapping caimans, you've got water weasels that will run up on those cats, you've got the homicidal feather duster that could one-shot both of them, and then you've got this tiny frog found only on the coast of Colombia that could probably solo the entire roster. Which means that at least once in history, the same jaguar that bullies a crocodile's little brother got put out of commission by a frog that could sleep comfortably on a quarter. I don't know who was working when this frog was made, but it was definitely on their last day.

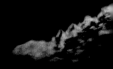

"And since its poison stops nerve impulses, not only can it make your heart file for unemployment, this murder Kermit could **TURN YOU INTO PAST TENSE IN LESS THAN TEN MINUTES.**"

GORILLA

FOUND IN: EQUATORIAL AFRICA
MERK RATING: 6

Gorillas look terrifying and they should—their bite force is off the charts. A motivated grizzly bear has a bite force of about 1,100 pounds per square inch; that's enough to crush a bowling ball. But gorillas have a bite force of 1,300 pounds per square inch. And who y'all call the "King of the Jungle" is literally half as strong, checking in at 650.

That mouthpiece is what helps them crush forty pounds of vegetation every day. To digest it all, gorillas have a massive amount of bacteria in their gut. This also means gorillas are almost always constantly farting. No, seriously, they don't stop. If there's a family of gorillas nearby, best believe you're gonna smell them way before you see them. And to make sure they get the most out of their diet, they've been known to drop a deuce in their own hands and eat it.

After defeating a rival, the male gorilla has been known to embarrass his competition by masturbating right in front of it, a very questionable power move. Not sure how that's a flex, because a 400-pound silverback gorilla can be packing about an inch and a half. Donkey Kong might be a unit, but he's packing less in his duffel than Toad.

But it's crazy what makes them squirm. This 300–400-pound live-action Donkey Kong is afraid of insects like caterpillars and reptiles, especially chameleons. Baby gorillas will play with almost anything but hit the brakes immediately the moment they see a lizard. Same dude you thought could take Godzilla gets sent packing by a bug. Now isn't that the very definition of irony.

On top of that, gorillas hate water, and they really hate rain. If a troop of gorillas gets caught in a storm, they'll just sit motionless and wait for the rain to pass. If there's a cave or some shelter nearby, they'll go in and hide. This is weird because gorillas will walk through swamps and babies will play in water, but rain is where they draw the line.

And finally, the sound of them beating their chests is something no words can possibly ever prepare you for. It's definitely not fierce.

GREAT WHITE SHARK

FOUND IN: COASTAL OCEANS WORLDWIDE
MERK RATING: 4

The face of Jaws has been terrorizing beachgoers for as long as we've known about great whites. But do they really deserve their label as fearsome killing machines?

Let's start with the facts. The great white shark can grow to more than twenty feet long and weigh in at up to 5,000 pounds of cartilage and attitude (and fun fact, the females are bigger). Obviously, their most famous feature is those 300 serrated, flesh-slicing blades for teeth. And great whites are estimated to have a bite force in the neighborhood of 4,000 pounds of force per square inch. That blows the 3,700-pound bite of the saltwater crocodile out of the water (pun intended). Those lethal jaws are designed to tear their prey to chunks that they swallow whole. But it's not just the shark's dental plan that makes them such feared predators.

Great whites, and sharks in general, have complex sensory abilities. They have an almost unnatural sense of smell, and are believed to be able to trace and track fish oil or blood from roughly a mile away. Unlike other fish, sharks have eyes with pupils that can dilate and contract to let different amounts of light in to help them see their surroundings. Which is why great whites will actually stick their heads out above water to observe what's happening, something very few fish do. Great whites also have a keen sense of hearing, and—fun fact—research shows that they are attracted to the sounds of heavy death metal. Why? Because it reminds them of the sound of struggling prey.

They're one of the most efficient killers in the waters, and if the homicidal Oreo called the orca didn't exist, they'd answer to nobody. But sharks are not nearly as dangerous as Hollywood makes them out to be, and it's mostly because we're not worth the effort. With our low body fat (at least compared to a sea lion) and general body composition, humans are basically brussels sprouts to them. In fact, most attacks are a result of sharks confusing us for sea lions. And statistically you are more likely to be turned into past tense by a falling coconut, a vending machine, or your significant other than by a shark. Yet I guarantee you'll still buy those Cheetos, and you'll still kiss your spouse.

" Great white sharks are such well-designed predators that they've been around for

400 MILLION YEARS,
LONGER THAN TREES AND
THE RINGS OF SATURN,

yet have more or less remained the same the entire time. "

GREEN ANACONDA

FOUND IN: AMAZON AND ORINOCO RIVER BASINS, TRINIDAD, GUIANAS
MERK RATING: 6

There are a lot of snakes in the world (you've probably dated some of them), but the biggest of them all is the green anaconda. Not to be confused with the reticulated python, which wins the title of the longest, the anaconda typically grows to fifteen to eighteen feet in length, and there have been reports of these snakes weighing in at well over 500 pounds.

Anacondas are constrictors, meaning it's not venom you'd have to worry about; it's the way they squeeze the life out of you and then swallow you whole. The anaconda is basically one huge muscle and, when wrapped around prey, it can deliver a hug strong enough to break ribs and collapse lungs. And once that happens, you probably know what's coming next. Like all snakes, the anaconda doesn't waste time chewing its food; instead it swallows the entire thing in one piece.

Contrary to what you may have heard, snakes like the green anaconda don't dislocate their jaws to feed. Instead, their lower jaw is separated into two halves that are connected by a stretchy, elastic-like ligament that allows the snake to open its mouth wider than your mental health can handle. It's the reason constrictor snakes can easily swallow something physically larger than their head. This nightmare ability, coupled with a nonexistent gag reflex, is how this absolute unit of a snake can swallow animals like capybara, peccaries, caiman, and deer.

To truly paint this picture, imagine being able to swallow a watermelon without chewing and with your hands tied behind your back.

Now if we're being fair to the snake, the likelihood of a snake swallowing a human has been drastically overblown by sensationalist media. Cases of snakes like anacondas eating people are very few and far between, and even the specifics on those cases are pretty murky. That being said, an anaconda that can allegedly deepthroat a jaguar without a second thought (or even a thought, period) should have no problem downing a human. And even though it's really, really, REALLY rare for one to even try, and the chances of it happening may be low . . . they're not zero. Just keep that in mind.

1

INLAND TAIPAN

On a scale from the Hudson River to Future's relationships, this snake is as toxic as toxic gets. One bite's worth of venom can kill 100 people and a quarter of a million mice. Taipan venom contains neurotoxins, hemotoxins, mycotoxins, and nephrotoxins. Basically if you get bit, you're fifty flavors of fucked.

2

EASTERN BROWN SNAKE

This highly venomous snake is regularly encountered by people. It's responsible for more than half of all snake bite fatalities in Australia.

FOUR SNAKES THAT ARE AS DEADLY AS THEY LOOK

4

KING COBRA

This apex predator often hunts other snakes, including its own species. Their venom contains neurotoxins that attack the nervous system and can lead to a complete shutdown. A human can die thirty minutes after being bitten. It's strongly believed the amount of venom injected in one bite is enough to drop an elephant.

3

BOOMSLANG

This dangerous snake, found in sub-Saharan Africa, is armed with a hemotoxin-rich venom that can cause life-threatening hemorrhaging in muscles and the brain. Symptoms usually don't appear for hours, which often makes people mistakenly assume the bite was dry and subsequently fail to get proper medical attention.

GRIZZLY BEAR

FOUND IN: NORTH AMERICA

MERK RATING: 8

Some people believe that a gorilla could take on a grizzly bear. Here are six reasons why this isn't even a debate:

1 **A male grizzly can be ten feet tall and weigh more than 800 pounds.** Leopards are about 130 pounds and they've been known to clap gorillas, so tell me again what they're gonna do with a bear.

2 A gorilla wouldn't even be able to high-five a grizzly because he'd go home with fewer hands than he woke up with. **A grizzly can turn a moose into a paraplegic with one slap, so it could easily one-shot any gorilla.**

3 A gorilla has no armor, just a six-pack and vibes. **Grizzly bears have a thick layer of fur, fat, and muscle that makes them damn near bulletproof.**

4 Gorillas aren't hyper-aggressive brawlers but are actually pacifists afraid of caterpillars and chameleons. **Grizzlies are 100 percent on sight with mountain lions, moose, and, worst of all, other grizzlies.**

5 **Grizzlies can reach speeds of thirty-five miles per hour.** Even though a horse can outrun them in a race, the bear's quick initial burst means it could catch a horse over a short distance. So whether the gorilla chooses to run or to fade, he's getting turned into a chalk outline regardless.

6 **The only advantage the Harambe disciple has is thumbs.** And unless he uses them to grab a Glock, he's getting clapped seven days a week and twice on Sundays, disrespectfully.

HARPY EAGLE

FOUND IN: CENTRAL AND SOUTH AMERICA
MERK RATING: 4

Yeah, this isn't Photoshop, that's a harpy eagle and yes, you should be afraid of it. Here's why the largest eagle in the world is an *Avengers*-level threat in the jungle. To start, harpy eagles have massive claws. Scientists have compared their talon strength to the jaws of a rottweiler. And since the harpy eagle has claws bigger than a grizzly bear's, they could barbershop grip a human head.

Also, nature did something incredibly out of pocket with them. Unlike most other eagles, harpy eagles have relatively short wings for their size, meaning they can bob and weave through the branches of the jungle. This also means this is the only eagle where hiding in the trees means nothing—you would still get worked, merked, and put on a shirt. Because of this, harpy eagles will make victims out of monkeys, sloths, opossums, or iguanas, and they'll even friendly-fire other birds, like macaws.

Even though it could probably hole-punch a human head, there are no reports of a harpy eagle ever killing or severely injuring a human. They're only really aggressive if you get too close to their nest—one look should tell you all you need to know about this steroid jungle pigeon. But if you do that and get clapped for it, at that point just charge it to natural selection.

In fact, because harpy eagles have zero fear of humans, it actually makes them an easy target for poachers. That and by gentrifying the jungle and knocking it down, we've destroyed a good amount of their home. So really, you're looking at one of the most dangerous destructive species in the jungle, and next to it is an eagle.

Fun fact: Harpy eagles mate for life, which means this feathery demon is still somehow more faithful than some, if not most, people.

THREE EXAMPLES OF EAGLES HAVING NO REGARD FOR LIFE

1. **Golden eagles** will grab goats and attempt to send them to the gulag by dragging them off a cliff to fall to their series finale. The birds apparently do the same with tortoises. However, getting a tortoise to come out of its shell involves air-dropping it from hundreds of feet in the air until it looks like an unfinished jigsaw puzzle. One eagle mistook the bald head of the ancient Greek playwright Aeschylus for a rock and dropped a tortoise on him, killing him.

2. **Bald eagles** will play chicken when they are horny. They flirt by locking their talons and performing a synchronized death spiral toward the earth. These eagles also actively flirt with death, because often they won't let go until the last possible second. Sometimes these flying derechos decide they don't value life and they won't let go at all. The result is that they get bird-smacked by the ground. This has to be one of the most metal ways to die.

3. **Sibling rivalry** for resources leads to homicide. Older eagle chicks will commit birdslaughter on a little brother while the mother watches the blood sport like a feathery sadist. Imagine getting merked by your sibling on your first day.

HIPPOPOTAMUS

FOUND IN: RIVERS AND LAKES OF SUB-SAHARAN AFRICA
MERK RATING: 10

Hippos aren't just the most aggressive animals in Africa, they're one of the most homicidal things to ever have a pulse. Not only can they clap crocodiles in half, these hell horses will merk animals that are literally zero threat to them. A hippo will straight-up Dahmer an antelope for no reason other than I guess the poor animal was breathing too loud and the hippo chose the death penalty.

They have one of the most devastating overbites of any animal, with a bite force of about 2,000 pounds. It helps that they're equipped with tusks that can grow to more than three and a quarter feet and are capable of punching through thick skin. And on top of that, the seemingly awkward hippo can run any human into the ground at speeds of thirty miles per hour. Also, fun fact, hippos are so dense that they don't really even swim as much as they just walk on the bottom of lakes. So when hippos chase boats, it's literally them sprinting underwater with malicious intent.

In an area code with elephants, hyenas, and buffalo, hippos are the most on sight, and they lay 500 people to rest permanently a year (at least). But God can't help you if they catch you in the water, because they've been known to capsize small boats and maul anyone that falls in. Don't think you're gonna get on their good side. One man adopted an orphan baby hippo, only to get brutally mauled and mutilated by the same hippo in the same river where he rescued it.

Moral of this entry: If you ever see a hippo yawn, you could be the one going to sleep.

THE MOST HOMICIDAL THINGS
TO EVER HAVE A PULSE. "

100 ANIMALS THAT CAN F*CKING

HONEY BADGER

FOUND IN: AFRICA, SOUTHWEST ASIA, INDIA
MERK RATING: 4

This animal is basically a Black Air Force One come to life. Honey badgers are mustelids, meaning they're related to weasels, otters, and wolverines. Basically we're dealing with a coked-out weasel with really bad 'roid rage. As the name would suggest, they love breaking into beehives and eating honeycombs. With crackhead determination, they'll continue to eat the honeycombs while being actively stung by hundreds of bees. Not because they're 100 percent immune to bee stings (they're only resistant). Nah, they just don't care.

And bees are the least of it. They'll take on and kill venomous snakes. A honey badger bitten by a snake will go into a coma, wake up several hours later, and just walk it off as if it were just a Sunday morning hangover. Also, they'll surplus kill. One once killed seventeen ducks and thirty-six chickens, and the crazy thing is he barely ate any of them. He was just stat padding at that point.

> **Two honey badgers were able to successfully fight off a pride of lions because EVEN LIONS KNOW YOU DON'T MESS WITH CRAZY."**

A honey badger's skin is tough enough to handle arrows, spears, porcupine quills, and even a strike from a machete. They also have really loose skin, so if a larger predator bites it, it'll turn around and attack the animal's face, because they don't run unless they're running fades. Plus, when threatened, this felony ferret will turn their anal pouches inside out, releasing a nasty skunk-like smell strong enough

to ward off most predators. And not only are they intelligent enough to use tools, they're smart enough to figure out how to escape from their zoo enclosures. Just ask Stoffel, who broke out of an African wildlife center multiple times.

And like the rest of its family, they have a nasty bite for their size, one that could even humble a tortoise. And of course we can't forget that they allegedly attack the baby makers of much larger animals, which is why this weasel can actually take on animals the size of a buffalo. Now can a honey badger kill a human? Not likely, but they have the tools to make your life absolute hell if you get on their shit list. You don't want a beef with an animal that lives life acting like it doesn't value life itself.

IRUKANDJI JELLYFISH

FOUND IN: WATERS OFF NORTHERN AUSTRALIA
MERK RATING: 9

Australia is a country with venomous snakes, rabbits that went to prison, actual devils, dinosaurs that we forget are dinosaurs, but the deadliest of them all is in the ocean. The Irukandji jellyfish is the most venomous thing on the planet, while also being small enough for you to never see it coming.

When this species of box jellyfish stings you, thousands of cells are injecting you with a venom that's 100 times worse than a cobra's and 1,000 times more potent than a tarantula's. You would feel extremely painful muscle cramps, a burning sensation on the face, vomiting, nausea, and headaches.

But that's not the worst part, because one of the symptoms of getting stung by this tiny jellyfish is an overwhelming feeling of impending doom so powerful that patients have been reported begging their doctors to take their life just to get it over with. You can feel all this in as little as five minutes. The pain is so excruciating that if you're swimming when the pain hits, you'll lose control of your body and sink to your death. The sting is so severe that it can even cause brain hemorrhaging, meaning you bleed from your brain. If it's treated quickly, you'll survive, but you'll be traumatized for life.

In a place where everything is evolved to kill you, this homicidal sperm cell, one that's less than half an inch in length, is the biggest opp of all.

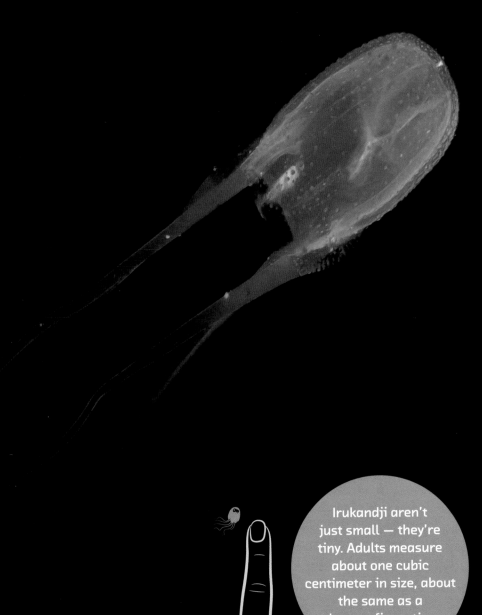

Irukandji aren't just small — they're tiny. Adults measure about one cubic centimeter in size, about the same as a human fingertip.

TINY ANIMALS THAT COULD TURN YOU INTO A HASHTAG

The **TSETSE FLY** transmits diseases that make the census half a million names lighter. One of these diseases is sleeping sickness, which not only can cause complete organ failure, it can severely alter your personality before you die. And if not treated, it could put you to sleep permanently as your body shuts down thanks to this OP-ass fly.

If you watch *Grey's Anatomy*, you know what time it is.

The **CANDIRU** is famous for allegedly swimming up the urethra of anybody with their junk out in the Amazon. You need surgery to remove them. It probably won't kill you, but the pain will make you wish it did.

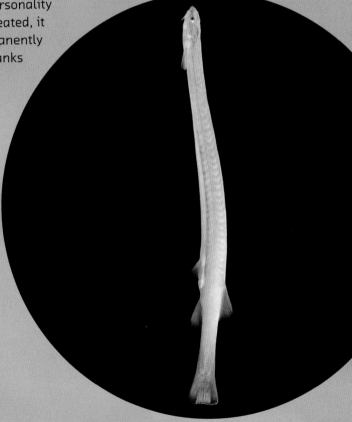

JAGUAR

FOUND IN: SOUTHERN ARIZONA, MEXICO, CENTRAL AMERICA, SOUTH AMERICA
MERK RATING: 8

Jaguars are literally everything leopards are but on steroids, the kind that get you banned for life. A jaguar can weigh more than 200 pounds (only lions and tigers are in a higher weight class), run at fifty miles per hour, climb trees almost as well as leopards, and look terrifying underwater. Now add the fact that they have night vision, camouflage, and some of them even come in black—meaning a jaguar could take your life before you even have time to realize you are in danger. Since there's no immigration control for a homicidal Garfield on PEDs, sometimes they end up wandering into the United States. Because they can climb, building a wall ain't going to do shit. Jaguars are a cheat code that God forgot to patch.

Jaguars regularly clap caimans by going into the water and dragging them out by their teeth like a disobedient child. That's because they do something that no other big cat does. Unlike lions, tigers, and leopards, which put their prey out of their misery by biting the neck, jaguars apparently watch *Endgame* and go directly for the head, which happens to be the caiman's weak point. And since this walking vise grip has the strongest bite of any cat (relative to its size) at 1,100 pounds per square inch, it puts the caiman in its coffin by biting through its skull and piercing its walnut-sized brain. The Amazon is one of the more dangerous places in the world and the Jaguar treats it like a supermarket.

MAMADOU NDIAYE

KANGAROO

Don't let the cute baby face fool you—kangaroos have psychopath tendencies. They will lead predators or humans to water and then force them underwater until they drown. One of their power moves involves holding you with their forepaws and then literally disemboweling you by kicking you with their claws. Their claws are sharp enough to leave your guts on the ground and your soul in God's inbox. And because a kangaroo's biggest enemy is the dingo, they're dog racist and will attack them just for breathing.

The worst thing you can do is feed them, because once you do, the grass-eating marsupials will expect and demand food from you. If you're empty-handed, they'll be disappointed. Disappointing an animal that looks like it just served ten in the pen could be bad for your health. One wildlife worker got kicked so hard, it broke her ribs and punctured her lung.

Also, weird fact: You know that thing that guys have one of and that different thing that girls also have one of? Yeah, female kangaroos have three and males' have two heads—I believe double-pronged is the expression. Only the alpha male kangaroo is allowed to mate, so the weaker males have to get creative, which is why sometimes they'll settle for sheep.

Plus kangaroos are responsible for 90 percent of animal-related car accidents in Australia. So basically, they're the deer of Down Under. But at least deer don't attempt to reverse baptize you.

HOW TO SURVIVE A KANGAROO ATTACK

1 **Don't look them in the eyes.** Actually rule of thumb, just don't look anything in the eyes—gorillas, kangaroos, parents—it doesn't lead to anything positive.

2 **Crouch down to appear as submissive as possible.** Stepping up to a kangaroo is a great way to get your kidneys kicked out. That right there is what you call a critical move, as in you'll be in critical condition if a kangaroo ever hits you with this two-piece with no drink.

3   **Cough.** To kangaroos, coughing is a sign of weakness and how an inferior male submits to the alpha male. So if this 'roid rabbit presses you and you don't cough, you'll be coughing up a lung.

4   **Have an object between you and the kangaroo.** I cannot stress this enough, you are not getting up if a kangaroo hits you with its kick—they are *One Punch Man* with kicking. All it takes is one hit to send you to all nine circles of hell.

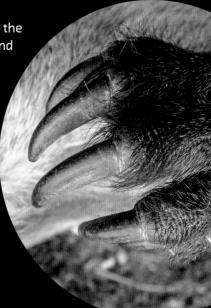

So yeah, crouch down, curl into a ball, don't make eye contact, cough, and question every life decision that led you to this point.

KOMODO DRAGON

FOUND IN: LESSER SUNDA ISLANDS OF INDONESIA
MERK RATING: 8

The world's largest living lizard takes its name from one of the islands in Indonesia where it lives. **If you find yourself trapped on that island, here's how you get out alive:**

- **Avoid the dense jungle**. Komodo dragons will hide in bushes just waiting for a chance to put you on the news. Young Komodo dragons can climb trees, so your best bet is to stick to the path.

- **Never be alone.** When Komodos select a target, they go for prey that's isolated and alone like a deer, goat, or a dumbass human that can't follow directions.

- **Don't try to touch one.** I didn't think I'd have to tell you why not socially distancing from an actual dinosaur is bad for your health, but a tourist got bitten by trying to take a picture with one.

- **Don't make any sudden moves or you'll trigger him.** Triggering a slightly nerfed Godzilla is a great way to get Ubered straight to God himself.

- **Don't wear perfume.** A Komodo dragon has a disrespectful sense of smell. Plus you're in the jungle—I don't know who you're trying to impress. If you're on your period, stay the hell inside. Komodos can smell even the slightest trace of blood. Once they do, they'll see you as prey and you'll have to pray to live long enough to see another day.

If a Komodo chases you, it means you've ignored everything I said and don't deserve or value the gift of life. **But if you want to fight natural selection, make sure you're running a zigzag, never a straight line.**

LEOPARD

FOUND IN: SUB-SAHARAN AFRICA, ASIA, RUSSIA
MERK RATING: 6

Leopards might be the most underrated big cat. They're not the biggest or the most famous, but they are one of the best-designed killing machines in Africa. Leopards have a prey base of nearly ninety animals, ranging from impala and gazelles all the way to gorillas, baboons, and even baby giraffes. And like most big cats, leopards finish their prey with a devastating bite to the neck. But it's what happens after the hunt that makes the leopard so impressive.

To avoid having to pay food taxes to lions or hyenas, leopards will carry their prey up into a tree where possible leachers can't reach it. And leopards can easily muscle an animal three times their size twenty feet up into a tree. In fact, if you see a young giraffe hanging from a branch, just know the number-one suspect was a leopard.

What they lack in bulk compared to heavyweights like tigers and lions, leopards compensate for by being the most agile. You can't outrun or outjuke a leopard, and trying to escape by climbing a tree

is a lot like running away from Michael Phelps but then jumping in a pool. Luckily, leopards usually don't see humans as food, and any attacks on people are typically territorial without predatory intent. This doesn't change the fact that they're serial killers with the grace and athleticism of an Olympic gymnast and the physical prowess of a weight lifter, all in a painfully beautiful spotted package.

LEOPARD SEAL

FOUND IN: ANTARCTICA
MERK RATING: 6

We aren't nearly as afraid of the leopard seal as we should be, because it's the second most homicidal thing in the Antarctic Ocean. In this case, "seal" stands for "Send your soul to Eternal Afterlife" (the L is sold separately). This murder puppy can grow to twelve feet long and weigh over 1,100 pounds. The leopard seal got its name thanks to his black spotted coat and the ability to merk almost anything in the water.

Since they're built like rubber submarines, leopard seals eat basically everything including fish, squid, and crabs. But if you watched *Happy Feet*, you know they save all the disrespect for penguins. They'll actually wait at the ice edge where they know penguins will jump in just so they can turn them into a hashtag. Sometimes they'll launch themselves out of the water onto land just to turn a penguin into a Happy Meal. In a single season, one leopard seal can erase hundreds of penguins, taking them out not for food but also seemingly for the stats. Sometimes it gets to the point where a mother leopard seal will bring an injured penguin to her inexperienced children to let the serial-killers-in-training get free practice—which has to be more insulting than just being eaten.

> **" And since leopard seals can swim twenty-three miles per hour, they're quick enough**
>
> **TO VIOLATE VIRTUALLY ANYTHING THEY WANT."**

But to be fair, they're not all bad. One leopard seal made friends with a photographer and brought him dead and injured penguins to try to teach him how to hunt. In seal society, that's as wholesome as you're gonna get. But that doesn't change the fact that they commit actual war crimes on penguins. If I showed you all the pictures, this would turn into a very different kind of book.

Oh, and you're not safe either. This underwater undertaker has been known to run fades with people, and one actually grabbed a scientist and mauled her underwater until she drowned. **When they pulled her out, she had more than thirty bites to the head and neck.** They've also been known to bite holes in inflatable boats filled with people.

LION

**FOUND IN: AFRICA
FROM THE SOUTHERN
SAHARA TO NORTHERN
SOUTH AFRICA
MERK RATING: 8**

Lions might not be the king of the jungle (queen is actually more accurate), but they're still terrifyingly dominant.

HERE ARE EIGHT REASONS WHY:

1. Lions are the only cats that roar together. They'll do it as a group for up to forty seconds to establish their territory and make every heart in a five-mile radius consider retirement.

2. Lionesses have two hunting positions. The fastest ones are called "wings," which guide the prey toward the lions in the middle, called the "centers." This strategy has a hunting success rate of 33 percent.

3. The worst time to get hunted by a lion is during a rainstorm. They can basically see in the dark, and the noise makes it impossible for you to hear them coming. So storms are when they're most successful and catch the most bodies.

4. Lions can accidentally lick your skin off because their tongue contains papillae designed to scrape meat off bones. Papillae is also the same stuff turtles have in their mouths.

5. They're freak athletes that can weigh 400 pounds, sprint at fifty miles per hour, leap thirty-six feet, and their triceps are top five. They have one weakness: They can only run in a straight line, which is why they get ankle-checked by gazelles

6 When a lion's hungry enough, it'll enter a state of psychosis and will attack literally anything for food even if it kills them. Which, in some instances, includes humans.

7 The males may be in charge, but the females will check them. The fastest way for that to happen is if he's being rough with the cubs. Lionesses have also been known to gang up on and merk elderly lions if they feel they're too old to run the pride.

8 Sometimes lionesses grow manes and they'll start acting like males, scent marking and humping other females. It's one thing we got wrong about lions: They're actually queen of the jungle.

MANTIS SHRIMP

FOUND IN: PACIFIC AND INDIAN OCEANS, WORLDWIDE
MERK RATING: 2

The mantis shrimp just makes no sense as a living animal—whoever designed it was on LSD. Let's discuss.

This shrimp can throw a punch at fifty miles per hour. God gave them the right to bear arms and they act accordingly. Not only can it throw hands faster than literally anything else on Earth, the punch's acceleration is basically the same as getting hit with a .22. Their punch is so quick that it causes a cavitation bubble to form. When it pops, it's hotter than the surface of the fucking sun.

Built like an underwater pride flag with the left hand of Thanos, the mantis shrimp hunts by repeatedly striking the shells of clams, snails, and crustaceans until they split open.

That pounding and the heat of getting pimp-slapped by Lucifer makes it easy for the mantis shrimp to turn its prey into a prayer. If it weren't for the fact that they can shatter aquarium glass, they'd actually be dope pets.

And that's not the only crazy thing about them. Their eyesight is so advanced that they can see polarized and ultraviolet light that's invisible to us. And where we have three color receptors, God said "Why not?" and decided to give this shrimp sixteen. They don't see more colors than we do (that used to be a common myth), but each row of photoreceptors is designed to detect a different kind of light. Oh, and they have 360-degree vision—'cause nature really pimped out this shrimp for no reason.

THREE SPIDERS THAT SHOULD SCARE YOU

BRAZILIAN WANDERING SPIDER

There are some spiders I don't forgive God for making, including the Brazilian wandering spider. It doesn't build a nest but actively hunts prey on the forest floor at night. If it wanders over to you, the bite from a Brazilian wandering spider can cause chest pains, heart palpitations, and vomiting. And because nature has a sick sense of humor, the bite also causes a painful, raging four-hour erection. This homicidal Cialis with legs can also cause impotence. So yeah, they take your sex life first, and your actual life second.

REDBACK SPIDER

I personally love spiders and believe that for most of them, their negative reputation is pretty undeserved. That belief does not apply to the redback, one of the most feared arachnids in Australia and, honestly, rightfully so. Not only do they have powerful, incapacitating venom, they have a habit of occasionally popping up in human homes. Which is probably why an estimated 250 redback spider bites are treated in Australia each year. Female redbacks in particular are pretty sluggish introverts that rarely leave their web, so bites usually happen when someone unknowingly sticks their hand somewhere, not realizing they're entering a dangerous spider's living room. There have also been cases of people using outdoor restrooms, only to get a redback bite in the worst possible place. Use your imagination.

SYDNEY FUNNEL-WEB SPIDER

This is one of those spiders that helps Australia live up to its hellspawn reputation. The funnel-web is one of the most venomous things with eight legs. And because of their hyper-defensive nature, funnel-webs maintain a tight grip on their victim and keep biting repeatedly until they're eventually flicked off. Unfortunately, by that time, this spider has likely delivered enough venom to kill you if you don't seek immediate medical attention. Small children are especially vulnerable after being injected, with one kid dying fifteen minutes after being bit.

" They have large fangs that not only cause significant pain, but ARE STRONG ENOUGH TO PIERCE YOUR FINGERNAIL."

MARABOU STORK

FOUND IN: SUB-SAHARAN AFRICA
MERK RATING: 4

I hate this bird based on its appearance alone. Not only can this demon have a twelve-foot wingspan, the marabou stork can be up to five feet tall, meaning they can look a good percentage of the population in the eye. If one does look you in the eye, you'll quickly find out they have no soul or goodwill behind those pupils. They eat everything, like literally everything. Technically they're scavengers that eat the dead, which is why they're nicknamed "the undertaker."

But best believe they'll snatch up anything that moves, including other birds, lizards, small mammals, and human children (don't worry, we will get back to that). They especially do flamingos dirty.

The reason they're bald is because they go neck-deep inside rotting corpses. Also this flying garbage disposal will feed on feces. But the marabou stork's favorite place to find food is in our garbage, which means two things: one, this dumpster Tweety actually likes being around humans, and two, they are not afraid of us, because marabou storks are highly aggressive and territorial.

According to urban legend, there are some children who got put in a box because they got too close to them. Instead of delivering babies, this stork returns them. With a beak like that, I believe it. I'm a grown man, but if I ever walked into a bathroom and had a five-foot testicle with wings looking back at me, I would back out slowly.

Moral of this story: The marabou stork is an *Avengers*-level threat to my mental health and a feathery antichrist whose vibe I will never fuck with.

That neck scrotum is actually a gular pouch. It's used to make noise to help attract a mate, so this Satan turkey can make more of itself.

Marabou storks' legs are white because they leak liquid ass all over themselves so that when it dries, it cools them off.

" Somehow this 'roid deer is actually

CLOSER IN SIZE TO AN ELEPHANT THAN AN ACTUAL DEER. "

MOOSE

FOUND IN: CANADA, NORTHERN UNITED STATES, NORTHERN EUROPE, RUSSIA

MERK RATING: 9.5

Moose are a problem. A picture of one pretty much started my TikTok career: The first animal video I ever made was dedicated to just how ridiculous they are. And what was true then is still true today.

At 1,500 pounds and seven feet at the shoulder, the moose is always gonna be one of those things God forgot to put a scale limit on. The average male moose is ten feet tall, about the same height as the basketball rim you probably can't touch.

Also, moose can swim, and they'll dive up to twenty feet deep in lakes to eat underwater plants. This means that at least once in the history of mankind, some guy encountered one underwater and probably never slept well ever again. His therapist now drives a Bentley.

Moose can also run through six-foot-deep snow at thirty miles per hour. Have you seen that video where a moose appears to be running on the surface of a lake? Either the water is shallow or that's Moose Christ—it's the Moosiah.

You know when they say you should never swerve to avoid hitting an animal 95 percent of the time? That's because that 5 percent is when this antlered Grim Reaper is on the road. On a scale from one to fucked, you're bunkmates with Weinstein when its entire body comes down on your windshield and crushes you. The moose might walk away, but you're not coming out of that without wings and a halo. No wonder Canadians are polite. Their landlords are moose and they pay taxes to geese. You'd be humble too.

HOW TO SURVIVE A MOOSE ATTACK

The obvious answer is to just not be around one. Stay the hell out of Alaska and Canada. Except . . . moose are found throughout America, so there's that. What you need to understand is that moose aren't afraid of anything. To be fair, when you can walk on water like Moose Christ and cripple cars, there's not gonna be a lot of things that put fear in your heart.

But if a moose makes a decision to subtract you from the human population, here's what to do: Back away. Find a tree or a building to hide behind and pray that Moosiah spares you. Curl into a ball. If the moose knocks you to the ground, you want to protect your head and organs. Yes, while the moose might stomp you out with the force of fifty Ray Rices, curling into a ball might save your life. Do not get up right away. If you get up after an attack while the moose is still around, he'll have no problem issuing a round two assault on your soul.

> **"** Oh, wrong title—should be "How to Make Peace with Your God. Because that's the best you can do if **THIS TANK WITH ANTLERS WANTS TO END YOUR LIFE. "**

If you see a baby moose, you need to exit the premises immediately. Baby moose are one of the most dangerous things in nature. Why? Seeing that means the next thing you might see is an 800-pound pissed-off mother . . . and the next thing you'll see is a white light. That's how these things happen.

I really hope you never need any of this advice. But if you do and it doesn't work out, you'll have a great story to tell at the heavenly gates.

What's also unsettling about them is when you see a moray, only the head is visible and most of its body is hidden in a burrow. So it can be hard to believe that moray eels typically grow to six feet long and the largest ones have grown to ten feet. In fact, the longest slender giant moray ever recorded was a nearly thirteen-foot middle finger of a fish.

MORAY EEL

FOUND IN: BAHAMAS, FLORIDA KEYS, WESTERN ATLANTIC OCEAN
MERK RATING: 3

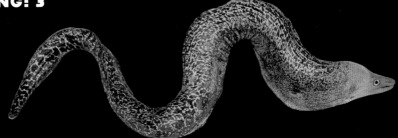

Is there a fish that looks more like a paralysis demon with gills than the moray eel? Those intimidating jaws definitely help make that case, but it's the jaws that you can't see that really make this eel so "special." Moray eels have a second set of pharyngeal jaws farther down its throat. Those jaws help ensure that anything unlucky enough to make it that far is definitely not getting out. And as opportunistic hunters, the "anything" can include fish, all the way to octopus and crabs. There's even been cases of a moray eel successfully eating a lionfish and unsuccessfully attempting to swallow a puffer fish. Being opportunistic basically means that if it fits down their throat, it's food. This attitude is why moray eels are considered apex predators.

However, as dangerous as this aggressive water Slinky can be, they are zero threat unless you happen to be a fish. Moray eels have never killed a person—the worst they'll do is deliver a nasty warning bite when you invade their space. And since these guys are typically nocturnal, the chances of you having a run-in with an angry moray are remarkably low. Which means you have to actually *try* to make them bite you. Moray eels, like a lot of things in life, are only really a threat to people stupid enough to provoke them.

MOSQUITO

FOUND IN: WORLDWIDE EXCEPT ANTARCTICA

MERK RATING: 10

Two things you should know:

1. Out of the more than 3,000 species of mosquitoes, it's mainly three (Anopheles, Culex, and Aedes) that are the most responsible for putting people under headstones.

2. And out of those three, it's only the females that are deadly because they are the ones equipped to draw and feed on our blood. They have two tubes that they inject into us, one to suck our blood and another to release an enzyme that inhibits blood clotting. The only problem is they often pass parasites directly into our bloodstream through their saliva. And that's where the nightmare starts.

Once the parasite has invaded your body, it feeds on the hemoglobin in red blood cells, destroying them. The more parasites that get pumped into your blood, the more red blood cells get compromised, which ultimately reduces your blood's ability to carry oxygen. And when the infected red blood cells burst, it only releases even more parasites to restart the process. Once that happens, you have now joined the list of millions of people infected with malaria. It's a crippling disease, one that has killed more people than every world war in human history combined. And that's not even mentioning the West Nile virus which, although it doesn't have the raw death count of malaria, is the most common cause of mosquito-related afflictions in the US.

OU NDIAYE

In terms of numbers, the mosquito is the deadliest animal to ever live, with a body count not in the thousands, but in the MILLIONS. It's estimated that this tiny buzzing Bundy is responsible for about one million obituaries every trip around the sun. And the most haunting part? They could easily be much more dangerous.

To add insult on top of incapacitating injury, we're not even a mosquito's first choice—it prefers to feed from horses and cattle. Matter of fact, a mosquito would likely choose a bird before you. So add the fact that only a small percentage of species can kill you and that only the females of those species can pass us the parasite with the disrespect of knowing we're not even their number one option. Oh and fun fact, Asian tiger mosquitoes (aka one of the few that can kill you) were accidentally transported throughout the world through shipments of tires. So we basically helped Uber the most notorious serial killers in history, proof that no matter how bad something is, you better believe humans will always find a way to fuck things up exponentially.

MOUNTAIN LION

FOUND IN: NORTH AND SOUTH AMERICA, FROM THE YUKON TO THE ANDES
MERK RATING: 6

God really should have drug tested mountain lions on their way out. Also known as cougars, they are a walking flex. I'm not even gonna acknowledge the fact that they look like they could deadlift my entire family tree or bicep curl my hopes and dreams. At seven feet long and around 200 pounds, I'm not sure if we're talking about a mountain lion or a damn linebacker. Ain't no way he's that cut without juicing.

It's crazy, you really can't run, climb or swim fast enough to not get violated by a cougar. Not only can they cancel your life, they can do it before it has a chance to flash before your eyes. They even dare to step to the Moosiah. Apparently, a male cougar managed to subtract the moose population by eighteen in less than a year.

> **" I haven't been this afraid of a cougar**
> **SINCE HAPPY HOUR**
> **AT APPLEBEE'S. "**

And strangely enough, they could very well be much more dangerous. But the truth is, mountain lions are much more afraid of people than we are of them, to the point that they'd be more likely to run away than try to fight you. But make them feel cornered or, worse, get too close to their cubs, and they'll introduce you to a whole new world of pain.

Did you know these PED pumas can leap forty-five feet? And if that doesn't sound impressive, it's because you haven't seen them in action. Not to mention they can run forty miles per hour, jump eighteen feet in the air, swim, and climb trees. You can't look at one move and tell me he's not on the same vitamins as LeBron James.

MUTE SWAN

FOUND IN: EUROPE, SIBERIA, UNITED STATES
MERK RATING: 5.5

Why does every swan on Google Images look so ready to throw hands on sight? These pond pigeons are what geese think they are. Because where geese are all talk, swans can actually do damage. The biggest is the mute swan, which can weigh more than thirty pounds and is strong enough to shatter your windshield if you happen to be at the wrong place at the wrong time.

You could try to humble a swan by grabbing its neck, but you're still risking your entire way of life if this angry Q-tip Tweety goes for your eyes. Geese are bullies, but it's mostly a defensive response. Swans are actually capable of putting you in an ER.

LOVE AND PIECES - OF YOU

Swans are supposed to represent love and peace, but they wake up and choose violence every day. A swan once attacked a man in a kayak, which capsized and he drowned. A swan once also killed a dog by beating it to death with its wings while its owners could only watch.

" The important thing to remember
is that swans are territorial and
**THEY ALSO HATE YOU AND
YOUR LOVED ONES ON A VERY
PERSONAL LEVEL.** "

ORCA

Sharks don't run the ocean—this steroid zebra guppy does. Their entire personality is bullying every name on the ocean census for no reason at all. Even though a wild orca has never caused a human obituary, some have started ramming into sailing boats off the coast of Spain and Portugal, damaging the boats and injuring the crews. The only reason they don't go after people is because they probably see themselves in us. Here's why this swimming sociopath is the most oppressive force in the entire ocean:

Orcas figured out that they can paralyze great white sharks by flipping them over. Once they do, they'll tear them apart and eat their liver and testes. They'll even bite off the tail fin so they can't escape. Sharks are so afraid of these murder dolphins that they'll abandon their hunting grounds for a year if they cross paths with an orca even once.

" They'll hacky-sack the poor seal until

ITS SKIN FALLS APART
AND ITS GUTS FLY OUT. "

Orcas are on record clapping moose swimming between islands. They play baseball with seals by slapping them up to eighty feet in the air. Sometimes they won't even eat the seal afterward, meaning this act of violation was purely for sport. They'll chase baby whales to exhaustion, tear their tongues out and eat the tongue, then leave the rest of the mutilated baby whale alone. Speaking of which, they'll pimp-slap stingrays to death for no reason, other than I guess they still haven't forgiven the one that took Steve Irwin from us.

Sometimes a mother and her son will team up to murder the baby of another female. Why? With the baby now a memory, the female is now free to mate with the son. So the mom commits homicide to get her son laid. Considering orcas are one of the most intelligent creatures on the planet, that was 100 percent malicious intent.

And even though they're built like an 8,000–12,000-pound equality symbol, they can launch themselves up to fifteen feet in the air. Really bad news if you're a bottlenose in the wrong place. And because this ocean Oreo has a range of almost everywhere, a grocery list of almost everything, their weaknesses only exist in fiction.

Conclusion: Willy should have never been freed.

TEXTBOOK HARASSMENT

Orcas will knowingly mess with other animals by creating waves that knock them off the ice. Sometimes they won't even eat the animal right away. They'll wait for it to climb back on the ice just so they can knock it down again in the world's most one-sided game of cat and mouse.

ANIMALS THAT LOOK DEADLY BUT AREN'T, PART 2

This LSD crocodile is a **GHARIAL** and, as a fish eater, it has zero interest in turning people into packs. And because they used to get hunted for their snout and skin, this acid trip water gecko is more afraid of us than we are of them.

Next is a paralysis demon with frequent flyer miles, the **ANDEAN CONDOR**. As scavengers with a weak beak and even weaker claws, they feed on the dead because they want no smoke with the living. No matter how ugly this flying testicle gets, they'll never attack a human. They're just out here minding their own business.

I know what you're thinking, but hear me out. **TARANTULAS** are almost zero threat to people because not only are they much more afraid of you, their bite is no worse than a bee sting. To my knowledge, they have never erased a person. The most dangerous thing about them is that they'll launch hairs at you if you get in their face. Other than that, they're one of those animals that look way worse than they really are.

The **GOBLIN SHARK** is a thirteen-foot hell guppy with a receding gumline that actually launches its jaw to catch prey. But they live at the bottom of the ocean, and they're way too lazy to be a threat to people if they didn't. They're blind, slow, and if looks could kill, they'd do Jack the Ripper numbers. But they're perfectly harmless.

And last is the **SHOEBILL STORK**. I'm not even gonna pretend like I haven't slandered the life out of this Jurassic Muppet. But the truth is they're really friendly toward humans and will even let bird watchers come right up to their nests without attacking them. And even though they look like a demonic hippogriff with the vocal chords of a machine gun, all you have to do is bow to earn their trust. For a bird that claps crocodiles for fun, this devil-like Tweety is just a feathery puppy.

OSTRICH

FOUND IN: AFRICA
MERK RATING: 7

While they are goofy looking, ostriches can kick with 2,000 pounds of force, which can cave your chest in and probably break a few ribs. Also, that long nail on its toe can disembowel you and cut arteries, causing you to bleed to death. And since ostriches can grow to nine feet tall, if one kicks you, the blow will land around your chest and stomach, which can easily cut your abdomen and spill out your guts. In fact, these overgrown sand pigeons have been known to merk lions. They don't have teeth, but they can still bite you hard enough to break skin. And at forty-three miles per hour, they're the fastest things on two legs. So if one decides to run you down, just hand your will to God, he'll file it for you.

But by far the most dangerous thing about ostriches is that they're stupid enough to find humans attractive and crazy enough to do something about it. Farm-raised ostriches have been known to ignore their own kind and make the kind of advances on people that would give you a workplace harassment lawsuit. Sometimes they don't stop at flirting and they'll actively try to deliver ten inches of hell. And that was not a joke—ostriches pack a ten-inch.

HOW TO SURVIVE AN OSTRICH ATTACK

Nine feet tall and over 300 pounds, this bird would literally bully a prime Shaq, and I'm supposed to tell you how to survive one? You could not beat an ostrich in a fight. You would get clapped, in more ways than one, disrespectfully. In nature, you typically have two options: Fight or flight. Since neither works with an ostrich, my only advice: Stay out of their way.

PEREGRINE FALCON

FOUND IN: EVERYWHERE EXCEPT NEW ZEALAND AND THE ARCTIC/ANTARCTIC
MERK RATING: 3.5

Peregrine falcons can max out at speeds of more than 240 miles per hour, making them the fastest animals in the world. This is really bad news if you're a pigeon, because they hunt by dive-bombing them feet first. This assault weapon with wings basically falcon-punches pigeons into the afterlife.

Falcons have two ways of catching bodies. Their first is simply chasing them. Since a motivated pigeon can change directions at sixty miles per hour, they can sometimes avoid them. Option two has the falcon start way up in the air, high above its prey, and begin to drop down like a feathery missile. They put their wings back into position called "the stoop," during which they can reach more than 200 miles per hour. But before a falcon soul strikes its victim, it opens its wings out like a parachute and hits the victim claw first, hard enough to shatter the bird's spine.

If a homicidal falcon decided to choose violence to bird smack you at top speed, it would either snap your neck or give you ten NFL seasons' worth of concussions. Because when it's on point, this might be the one Falcon on the planet that doesn't blow leads—I'm looking at you, Atlanta.

Falcons go so fast that their brains are designed to process images at ridiculous speeds. So when they're not turning themselves into weapons of mass destruction, falcons basically see everything in slow-motion.

MAMADOU NDIAYE

PITOHUI

FOUND IN: NEW GUINEA
MERK RATING: 6.5

Found in New Guinea, the hooded pitohui has concentrated batrachotoxin in its skin, feathers, and tissue, making it one of the few toxic things with wings. Batrachotoxin is the same toxin that makes the dart frog arguably the most poisonous creature on Earth. And just like the frogs, these toxic Tweetys get their biological weaponry from their diet of beetles.

The pitohui's poison not only protects it from predators, it also reduces its parasite problem. But could this built-in bug spray kill a person? Probably not. The neurotoxin is definitely a game over for something like a mouse, but for a healthy adult human, it's not likely to fall into the neighborhood of life threatening. However, if you have allergies, there's always a chance exposure can lead to anaphylactic shock. So even though it *probably* won't hurt you, the chances are never zero.

❝ Here's a friendly reminder
THAT NATURE MADE
POISONOUS BIRDS
and expects us to just be okay with it. ❞

PLATYPUS

FOUND IN: EASTERN AUSTRALIA
MERK RATING: 5.5

Platypuses make no sense, but they still can mess you up. Male platypuses (I refuse to say platypi, it sounds pretentious) are equipped with a sharp ankle spur designed to release painful, borderline incapacitating venom into anyone who poses a threat. This venom is more powerful than morphine, and the residual pain can persist even months after you've been stung. Yes, I said months. And since the toxins are more potent than morphine, there isn't a lot you can do to stop the pain.

Male platypuses use this spur against other males when fighting over territory or females. But that doesn't mean they won't extend the unpleasantries to handsy humans or unaware dogs.

> **" One thing is certain, though. Once you've been stung by this duck rabbit,**
> ## YOU WILL *NEVER* FORGET IT. "

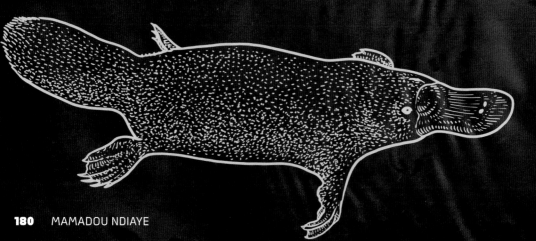

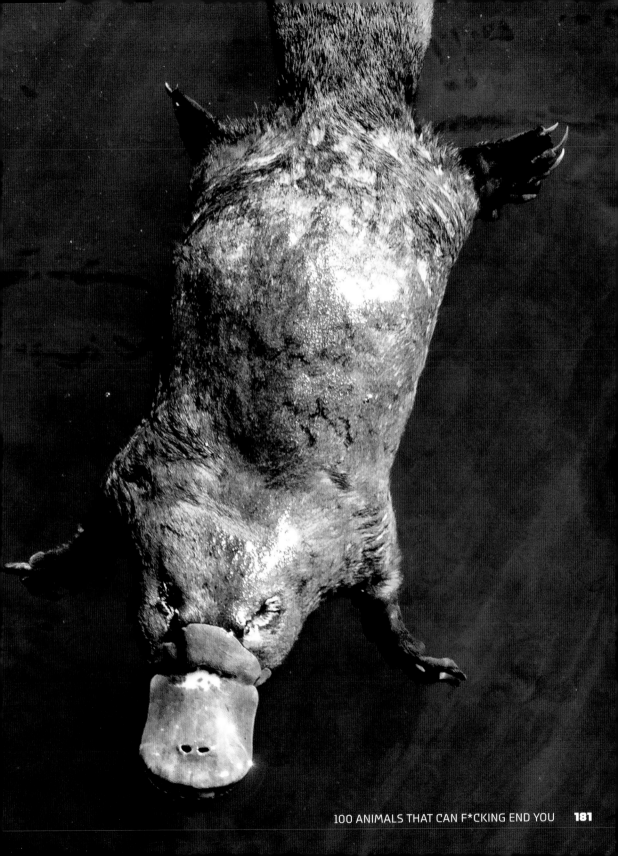

HERE'S A FEW MORE THINGS THAT MAKE THE PLATYPUS WEIRD

- They're beavers with duck bills and webbed feet that somehow lay eggs.

- They also produce milk but somebody forgot to give them nipples, so they sweat milk through their armpits.

- They don't have teeth, so they use rocks to chew their food.

- They're the only mammal that doesn't have a stomach, because they lost the genes for it.

- They're also the only mammals that use the power of electroreception, which is what sharks use to hunt.

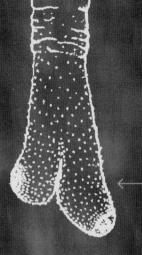

- They have a two-headed penis.

- They can track their prey through their heartbeat because that duck bill can detect electrical impulses.

- Since they close their ears and eyes underwater, they swim blind and deaf.

- They sleep more than sloths.

- They glow in the dark because . . . of course they do. They're a bluish green under UV light, meaning Dan Povenmine clearly knew something we didn't.

- They poop, pee, and give life out of the same hole. Scientists found this so fascinating that they named their entire family Monotreme (single-opening) after it.

- They use their tail to store fat reserves like camels use their humps.

❝ You know how we have two sex chromosomes? WELL, THESE GOOSE FERRETS HAVE TEN. ❞

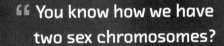

"POLAR BEARS ARE ONE OF THE FEW ANIMALS THAT WILL ACTIVELY HUNT HUMANS.

And once the hunt is started, it only ends when you do. "

SMELLS LIKE DINNER

Since polar bears live in a desolate, air-conditioned hell, nature gave them a nose that can smell a seal from a mile away and through three feet of ice.

POLAR BEAR

FOUND IN: ARCTIC OCEAN AND SEA ICE
MERK RATING: 10

The polar bear earns the heavyweight title as it is the largest land predator on the planet. What with them regularly weighing more than 1,000 pounds and standing up to eleven feet tall, there isn't a force in nature that can save you once this Caucasian carnivore decides to make you a statistic. Unlike most other bears, the polar variety is a hypercarnivore, meaning most of its diet consists of meat. None of that vegetarian nonsense for them; polar bears thrive off the blood of others.

Polar bears have a sense of smell believed to rival a bloodhound's, and they use it to sniff out their next meal. And since polar bears will travel miles for a possible meal, if one pulls up on you in the wild, there's a good chance it's been plotting on you for DAYS.

Black bears can be intimidated into running off. Playing dead with a grizzly can convince it that you're not enough of a threat for it to attack. Polar bears . . . yeah, I got nothing, you're unequivocally, exponentially fucked. "Just play dead." The polar bear is also a scavenger that'll have no problem eating you alive. "Make yourself look bigger." All good until the ice bear stands up and is tall enough to hit his head on a basketball rim. Can't run, polar bears have snowshoes for paws and can sprint at twenty-five miles per hour. Can't outswim them either since a polar bear can freestyle for miles at six miles per hour. Honestly, my only advice for a polar bear attack is to make peace with the higher being of your choice before the bear sends you there, toll free.

Standing up to 11 feet tall, this ice bear is tall enough to hit his head on a basketball rim.

SIX ANIMALS YOU DIDN'T KNOW WERE CANNIBALS

1. **Prairie dogs** will abort the babies of their relatives to lower the competition, which I guess is fine. But these prairie puppies take it a step further by eating the children they just spawn-wiped.

2. Adult **Komodo dragons** have cannibalistic tendencies, which is why hatchlings often spend time in the trees to avoid getting eaten by their own kind.

3. **Red squirrels** are vicious baby-killing cannibals that will wipe out entire nurseries, sometimes eat them, and then find a now-childless mother to try to re-create the family they just erased.

4. Imagine being merked by a twin before you're technically even alive. The first baby **sand tiger shark** to develop will swim around and cannibalize its little baby brothers and sisters while still inside the mother's uterus. This kill streak means that even though he technically has siblings, he's always born an only child, and that's just fucked.

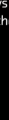

5 **Ladybugs** are also on that type of time. The first ones to hatch will immediately eat the eggs of their unborn siblings. Their first day of life they stat pad spawn kills. The ladybugs that put their own siblings on shirts develop faster, so nature actually rewards this psychopathic behavior.

6 Mother **hedgehogs** will make a pack out of the pincushions she calls children. They do this if they sense a disturbance, which isn't much of an exaggeration. They go from zero to life sentence if they don't like the weather.

SEA SNAKE

FOUND IN: INDIAN AND WESTERN PACIFIC OCEANS
MERK RATING: 7.5

Apparently, there are a lot of people who didn't know there are snakes in the ocean. I'm not talking about your ex at the beach, I'm talking about the venomous-toxic-kill-you kind. Yeah, that didn't really narrow it down.

Sea snakes are an actual thing—there are almost sixty species of them. After years of plot development, they've adapted and live in the ocean where they honestly have no business. Because they have larger lungs than normal, some of them can hold their breath for eight hours. Clock in for a shift at work and you can head home before this snake needs to come up for air. That's because some of these snakes can absorb oxygen through their skin. Also, these snakes can dive up to 300 feet straight down because . . . of course they can.

And because that obviously isn't terrifying enough, some of the most venomous snakes on the planet are actually the ones in the ocean. And then you have the **BLACK BANDED SEA KRAIT**, whose venom is ten times stronger than a cobra's. They're naturally shy, though, so they won't attack you unless you honestly give them a reason. But when you have the power to put an entire family reunion in the dirt, the least nature can do is make you an introvert.

But the biggest OP of all is probably the **BELCHER'S SEA SNAKE.** They're not super dangerous because they rarely bite, and when they do they don't release all their venom. That being said, because it's the most venomous snake in the ocean, one could put 100 men in coffins with one bite. Symptoms after getting bitten include muscle pain, tongue swelling, convulsions, and eventually becoming a story on the nine o'clock news. Yeah, not a gamble you want to take if you ever see one of them out in the ocean.

An **OLIVE SEA SNAKE** is toxic enough to put sixty men into God's recently deleted.

SECRETARY BIRD

FOUND IN: SUB-SAHARAN AFRICA
MERK RATING: 3

Secretary birds kill prey by kicking them in the head until they either tap out or flatline. They especially violate snakes, river dancing on their heads until their skulls cave in. The secretary bird can kick with a force five times its own body weight. That's like the average man Ronaldoing someone with 900 pounds of force. Their kick is so powerful that they can actually shatter the bones in your hand. Also, they're like four feet tall and can fly.

The secretary bird will stomp around vegetation and bushes just so they can skull check anything that tries to escape. They'll also purposely wait around bushfires so that if any small animal tries to run for its life, this bird will take it by curb stomping them. They can kick their prey in fifteen milliseconds, meaning in the time it takes for you to blink, they can strike multiple times. Like I said, they're 100 percent on sight with snakes because they'll smash their heads in until they're either paralyzed or dead and then proceed to eat them.

And they do all this while looking like a recently divorced velociraptor that got out of pocket with the child support. This is not a bird, it's *Jurassic Park* in yoga pants. Next time someone tells you dinosaurs are extinct, just remember this African homicide chicken tap dances on the graves of snakes and anyone else that tries to test it.

YOGA MOVES

The secretary bird can kick with a force five times its own body weight.

Unlike American black bears, who would rather run from a fight, sloth bears are all about the action. Armed with a set of claws and a nasty bite, a motivated sloth bear will occasionally hand L's to tigers, especially if its children are involved.

SLOTH BEAR

FOUND IN: INDIA
MERK RATING: 7.5

Put a wolverine on creatine, give it the personality of a power tool, and you get the sloth bear. This, in my opinion, is the most dangerous bear in the world, because it may not be the biggest but it's the most likely to press you for no reason. They wake and choose bodily harm, and their method of attack is going straight for the face, mauling you so severely that you become a stranger to your mother and iPhone. Sloth bears don't need fire to apply smoke and they don't need clippers to run fades.

And at five or six feet long, 300 pounds, with a top speed of thirty miles per hour, they could violate you in the jungle and the NFL combined. They can also swim and climb trees like a 'roid squirrel. They don't use this to get away from a fight, though, because animals that they run the ones with, like leopards, can climb too.

As insectivores, they typically eat termites and ants, which is great news for us. Because one time a sloth bear developed a taste for humans, and he put twelve people on shirts and another two dozen in the hospital. But getting mauled by a sloth bear has got to be one of the most painful ways to go. Tigers and leopards are at least hardwired to go for the neck and make it quick. A sloth bear will rearrange your face with those claws and then chew your arms and legs to a pulp, all while you're still alive. Baloo from *The Jungle Book* feels a little different now, doesn't he?

SPERM WHALE

FOUND IN: OCEANS WORLDWIDE
MERK RATING: 8.5

What if I told you there's an animal that could kill you without ever touching you? This is proof that the entire ocean needs a nerf. Sperm whales are the loudest mammals on Earth, producing sounds that can reach 230 decibels. I'm not gonna bore you with numbers, just know that 150 decibels can burst your eardrums. Jet engines are 140. Now you might think that's not as bad because they're in the water. I mean, you're right, but not really. Because even underwater these semen whales can produce at least 175 decibels. Death threshold for sound is 185 to 200, so if it doesn't send you to your ancestors, it definitely gets you closer to them.

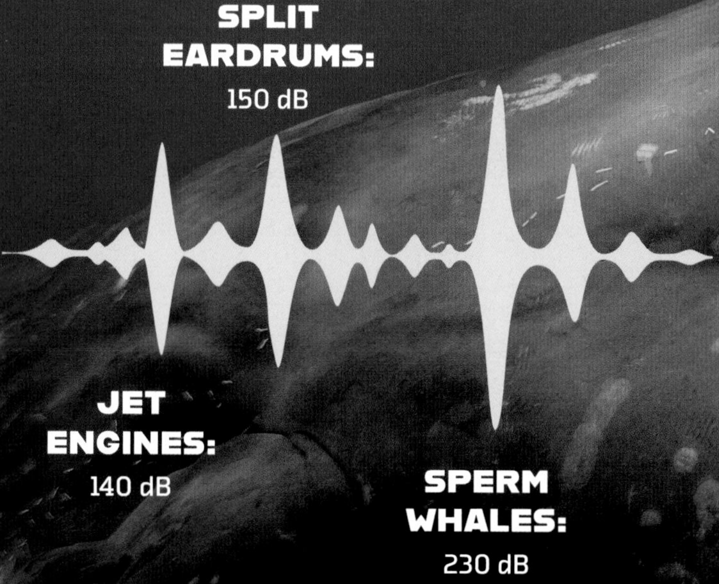

SPLIT EARDRUMS:
150 dB

JET ENGINES:
140 dB

SPERM WHALES:
230 dB

Luckily, sperm whales don't use this power for lethal force. They use it to communicate and understand their surroundings. Don't get it twisted, though. Sperm whales saying hello could still be your game-over because they make a sound loud enough to cause an embolism in your lungs, which can travel to your heart. At that point you'd be doing the mannequin challenge, permanently.

The moral is don't piss off a sperm whale. Because if he raises his voice, your soul will ascend and your body won't come with it.

NORMAL THINGS THAT ANIMALS DO THAT WOULD KILL YOU

If you hung out with a group of **FLAMINGOS**, you would die. The water they stand in is so toxic that it would strip the skin off your legs in seconds and probably burn a hole in your throat.

The **CLICK BEETLE** launches itself in the air with a force of 400 G's. In case you were wondering, ten G's can cause you to lose consciousness and twenty can evict your soul from your body permanently. They may be small, but no other animal can handle that kind of force. And a fraction of that will turn you into past tense.

The **BHARAL SHEEP** live high in the Himalayan mountains. They can live 17,000 feet high on cliffs where one slip means stage fatality. But the thing is, they don't slip. In fact, they'll actively try to yeet each other off the mountain. If you lived here and didn't fall to your season finale, you'd either freeze to death or suffocate. Trying to breathe that high up is like trying to breathe through a straw while on a treadmill.

The **WETA** is the most hardcore cricket you'll ever find. When it gets too cold, they'll straight-up freeze solid. And when the ice melts, they walk it off like it's nothing. Their heart and brain literally stop, as all the water in their body becomes ice. When ice forms in your body, it destroys every cell it touches. And even if you warm up, those cells are gone. But when you give Jesus plot armor to a cricket, this is what you get.

The **GANNET** will dive from over 100 feet and hit the water at sixty-two miles per hour. If you tried that, you would probably shatter every bone in your body. Gannets have built-in airbags to absorb the shock. But since you don't, hitting the water that hard would factory reset your soul.

SPOTTED HYENA

FOUND IN: SUB-SAHARAN AFRICA
MERK RATING: 9

How do you survive a hyena attack? After extensive research, I came to the conclusion that if you put yourself in a position where a hyena decides your fate, you don't deserve to be alive to waste our oxygen supply.

That might seem harsh, but we're talking about an animal that will step up against Simba, Mufasa, and whoever they put in a new kids' remake. I know what you're about to say—it takes like twenty hyenas to take down a lion, right? Gang violence is a problem everywhere, but it reaches its peak here because hyena clans can reach up to eighty members, and every single one will violate you with extreme prejudice. Hyenas have been known to mob other predators and steal their kill. (Although their reputation as scavengers has been unfairly overblown, since 70–90 percent of their meals consist of animals they actually hunted and killed.)

You can't run. They'll chase you down at thirty miles per hour over three miles. That's being run down by the hyena mafia for the length of 264 football fields.

You can't play dead because pretty soon you won't be able to play alive. Fun fact: They usually start meals by tearing through the abdomen and pulling out the intestines. All while you can only lie there and wait for your ticket to the afterlife to get punched.

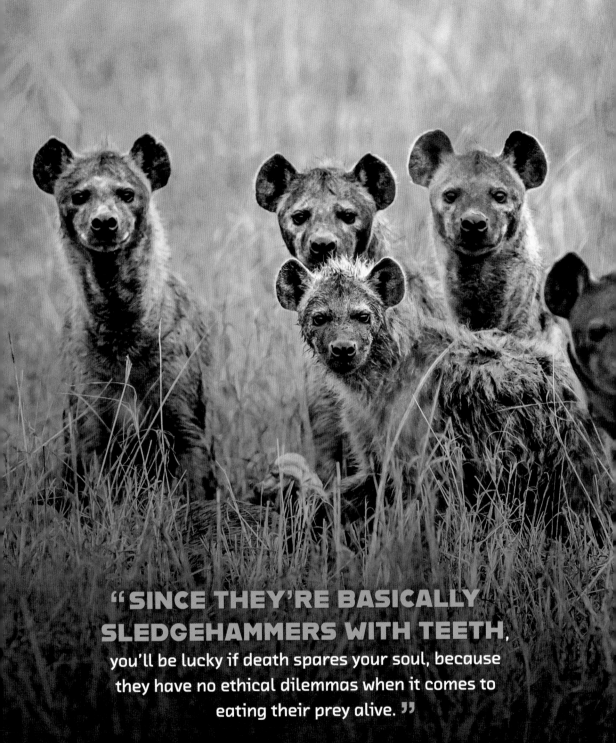

"SINCE THEY'RE BASICALLY SLEDGEHAMMERS WITH TEETH, you'll be lucky if death spares your soul, because they have no ethical dilemmas when it comes to eating their prey alive. **"**

Let's talk about those jaws. With one of the strongest bites of any land carnivore relative to body size, hyena teeth are engineered to tear through flesh and crack bone. That is a mouthpiece that could amputate a full-grown rhinoceros.

They can snap your leg the same way we bite into celery, and since their teeth are covered in rotting flesh, even if you survive, the infection you'll get will make you wish you hadn't. You don't want those problems. Let's not forget how *Lion King* ended.

Hyenas are one of the toughest animals on the plains. They have to be, since they quite literally come out of the womb fighting. That's not hyperbole either. Newborn hyena cubs will immediately start fighting the other siblings in the den. This isn't cute play-fighting—hyenas are born with their eyes open, a full set of teeth, and the females are flush with testosterone. That aggressive nature is why one in every four hyena cubs born will never make it out of their birth den.

With that kind of childhood, it's not surprising that they grow up to become one of the most feared predators in Africa. When these brutal carnivores live in close proximity with humans, they have been known to subtract an estimated fifty people a year and injure many more. There have been reports of hyenas breaking into people's homes and pulling people out of bed to NyQuil them permanently (seriously, it happened in 2020).

Do hyenas deserve the nasty reputation they've gotten? Of course not. What Zazu called "slobbering, mangy vultures" are actually highly intelligent, efficient pack hunters that are doing what comes naturally. Doesn't change the fact that they'll turn you into a chalk outline with zero hesitation.

STELLER SEA LION

FOUND IN: NORTHERN PACIFIC OCEAN
MERK RATING: 6.5

Sea lions are freaking units. The biggest of all is the Steller sea lion, which can violate the scales at as much as 2,000 pounds. Only two things can check them: Jaws and Freed Willy.

Everything else is a victim because that's what they eat—everything else. Stellers eat all types of fish, squid, and octopus, but they'll also add seagulls, fur seals, and baby sea otters to the list. And even though we call them sea lions, if you really want to be a nerd about it (and you know I do) the pinniped group that they're part of is actually closer to bears, meaning this guy's closer to being a sea grizzly than a sea Simba.

And since they're basically breast stroking water bears, they have a similar jaw structure, which is why social distancing from a sea lion might be good for your health. Because at ten feet long, a motivated Steller sea lion can and will bite clear through your arm. And since they eat seafood without ever seeing floss, you will 100 percent get an infection. They've been known to turn their own children into memories, just so they can mate with their mother. They barely have any regard for their own kind, what makes you think they won't turn on you?

"IT'S BUILT LIKE A WASHING MACHINE WITH FLIPPERS."

STINGRAYS

FOUND IN: COASTAL TROPICAL AND SUBTROPICAL WATERS WORLDWIDE
MERK RATING: 3

Okay, I should probably start with Steve Irwin. In 2006, one of these homicidal water placemats took the beloved wildlife expert away from us forever with a devastating venomous barb to the chest.

But stingrays aren't nearly as dangerous as you'd think. They don't use their venom to hunt, but only for self-defense as a last resort. Because unless a stingray's life is in jeopardy, it would rather swim away than waste biologically expensive venom. Most people who get stung have nearly stepped on the stingray without even realizing it. (Some people would do the same if you almost stepped on their new sneakers.) With antibiotics, stingray venom is rarely, if ever, life threatening.

Which of course brings us back to Khaki Jesus, aka Steve Irwin. As tragic as it was, his death was more of a freak accident than anything. He was wounded right in the chest, specifically in the thoracic wall, while he was exploring a reef. Meaning he wasn't close enough to land to receive the medical treatment that would've saved him. Also, Steve Irwin was notorious for interacting with venomous animals without carrying antivenom. There were also reports that Irwin pulled the barb out of his chest himself. Now, I'm not a doctor

(Organic Chemistry 101 guaranteed that I never would be), but I'm pretty sure that didn't help. So it took getting stung in the worst possible spot, in a place with no immediate access to medical attention, with no antivenom on hand, for a stingray to cause a fatality. But knowing him, the last thing he would've wanted would be for us to villainize stingrays for it.

The haunting irony is that a man who regularly came into contact with crocodiles, snakes, and spiders (not to mention people) ended up falling to an animal that really shouldn't have been that dangerous. Stingrays are natural pacifists that, in a world of fight or flight, would rather swim away from their problems.

Stingrays' venom can cause you to feel extreme pain, nausea, weakness, with the worst and final symptom of erasing all feelings permanently. Every year, stingray encounters send people to the emergency room, often while in agonizing pain.

STONEFISH

FOUND IN: COASTAL INDIAN AND PACIFIC OCEANS
MERK RATING: 8.5

The fish you should be most afraid of certainly isn't the stingray, it's the stonefish. This fish is armed with a venom called verrucotoxin. As a neurotoxin, it shuts down your body from the inside. If you get stung, you first feel incapacitating pain, swelling, and eventually numbness. But no worries, it gets worse—it always gets worse.

> " Its spines can deliver venom powerful enough to cause crippling pain and toxic enough to activate your life insurance in **LESS THAN TWO HOURS.** "

If you don't get medical attention fast enough, the poison will destroy tissues in the body, cause uncontrollable twitching and shaking, and eventually paralyze you. This means it will get harder and harder to breathe until you eventually black out. Victims describe the pain as like getting continuously hit with a jackhammer all over the body. Even if you survive, you can still walk away with permanent nerve damage and muscle atrophy.

Can you even find this thing in the image on the right? Stonefish camouflage isn't just deadly to their prey; people swimming in coral reef habitats who step on or brush against them can catch their death without even knowing what stung them.

THERE ARE TWO BIG REASONS WHY THIS SATAN GUPPY MIGHT BE THE MOST DANGEROUS FISH ON EARTH:

1. The stonefish looks like a stone. It's so easy to accidentally step on one, and when you do, those spines get shoved up your foot. The harder you step, the more poison gets pumped into you.

2. They can survive outside of water for up to twenty-four hours, meaning they don't have to be underwater to put you underground.

FOUR MORE REASONS NOT TO GO IN THE WATER

1

THE NEEDLEFISH
MERK RATING: 6

This scaly hellspawn will heave itself out of the water at thirty-seven miles per hour with no regard for the welfare of anybody around it. This kamikaze with gills has been known to stab people in the face. A ten-year-old boy once got pierced through his eye and into his brain. One woman got stabbed above the eye. Take a wild guess where you can find this guy? No, no, take your time. Yeah, Florida.

2

AFRICAN TIGERFISH
MERK RATING: 5

This Satan's goldfish will not only attack people but it will eat crocodiles too. It's an overgrown, 'roided-up piranha with an overbite. Also, African tigerfish can catch and kill birds in flight. God did not vault all his mistakes, and this is the proof. Unfortunately, its aggressive behavior makes the tigerfish a popular (and illegal) pet for some people.

3

JAPANESE SPIDER CRAB
MERK RATING: 1

There is no ethical reason for this animal to exist. The Japanese spider crab can have a leg length of twelve feet, weigh forty-four pounds, and live for 100 years—because even death procrastinates dealing with this thing. But other than being a threat to your mental health, this massive spider crab is virtually harmless, since it's an obligate scavenger that prefers to make a Happy Meal out of dead animal and plant matter it finds on the ocean floor. If you have a pulse, you're probably not its type. While you have nothing to be afraid of, your therapist might be able to retire early if you ever see this thing in person.

4

PORTUGUESE MAN-OF-WAR
MERK RATING: 7

The Portuguese man-of-war is also known as a blue bottle, also known as a floating terror. It's a species of siphonophore armed with millions of explosive stinging cells powerful enough to make Nemo an orphan and occasionally turn a person into past tense. This man-of-war is responsible for up to ten thousand stings in Australia alone. The venom can cause excruciating pain for up to three days, leaving a nasty whiplike welt as a souvenir. But honestly, you're lucky if that's all you get, because the venom can trigger an allergic-like reaction that results in throat swelling, heart issues, and difficulty breathing causing you to suffocate, possibly to death.

FUN FACT:

A man-of-war can write your obituary days after becoming one itself. Even tentacles that have been separated from its body contain enough venom to incapacitate you.

STRIPED ANEMONE

FOUND IN: AUSTRALIA
MERK RATING: 4.5

This Oreo-colored body snatcher is the *Dofleinia armata*, a striped sea anemone. The largest type of anemone, it's found off the coast of . . . I don't even need to tell you, you know it's in Australia. The only thing you need to remember is to stay the God-fearing fuck away from this thing because not only can it sting you, it can incapacitate you for months. These anemone are part of the *Cnidaria* family. I'm not even finna lecture you—the only names you need to remember are jellyfish and man-of-war, because those are its cousins.

Their tentacles have papillae covered in large, explosive stinging cells called nematocysts, which will introduce themselves to your skin if the satanic Pokémon feels threatened. The tentacles end with a swollen tip that's also covered in excruciatingly painful venom. The difference between this thing and your ex, if bro hits you with just the tip, you'll actually feel it. And you can continue to feel it for up to several months because, of course.

I actually love Australia, but this is just more evidence that the entire country is just one of one.

WILD BOAR

FOUND IN: EUROPE, ASIA, NORTH AFRICA
MERK RATING: 8

Wild boar are a special kind of menace to society. When they choose the death penalty, they charge and impale you with those daggers they call teeth. Then they'll take a step back and, if you are still moving, they'll rush you again. They'll keep doing this until you are either crippled or a was.

Boars have the homicidal tendencies of hippos with the street smarts of raccoons. This steroid Porky has learned to stay close to humans because our garbage is basically free food to them, which is why they'll easily take your soul over half a box of popcorn. And according to cave paintings, they've been on our ass since the Stone Age. But like everything else, this is our fault. Because the more we move into their hood, the more they lose their natural fear of humans, and the more obituaries get cosigned by this truffle demon.

" The biggest ones can weigh up to 400 pounds **WITH TUSKS THAT CAN PUT YOU IN A NEWSPAPER.** "

And once again, Florida goes to hell and brings the bar with it. They're an invasive species and there's not 1,000, not 5,000, but half a million of these rogue pigs in the Sunshine State, to the point where they might start voting in the next election. But don't feel too bad: Texas has about 2 million of them. You can find feral hogs in about thirty states. God gave them life, and they make it everyone's problem.

When a wild boar attacks, it usually aims for the thighs, so if they sever your femoral artery, it's curtains my guy.

WOLF

FOUND IN: CANADA, NORTHERN UNITED STATES, EUROPE, ASIA
MERK RATING: 4

In my opinion, there might not be an animal that we've done more dirty than the wolf. As if an undeserved man-eating reputation wasn't bad enough, it nearly led to the gray wolf being completely wiped out in America. Luckily, they've made a comeback, both in terms of population and in terms of their perception by the general public. But in case some of you reading still think wolves are vicious killers, read on.

" THE BIG BAD WOLF IS TERRIFIED OF PEOPLE, and considering the number we did on their numbers, they're not exactly wrong. "

Wolf attacks are incredibly rare, and records of wild wolves mauling a person are few and far between. If one does happen, it's almost definitely defensive, since wolves don't associate us as part of their usual prey. Wolves are literally the epitome of "they're more afraid of you than you are of them."

Another piece of wolf misinformation that's pissed me off for years is there is no such thing as an "alpha wolf." There are no violent disputes for control of the pack, and that's because a wolf pack is really just an extended family made up of two parents and generations of their children. The "alphas" of the pack are literally just the wolves that birthed and sired the others. And to avoid senseless fights, wolves use complex vocalizations and body language to communicate to the other members of the pack. So situations rarely have to devolve into violence, meaning an animal that can't talk is better at using their words than some people.

But could a wolf kill a human? Yes, and it's almost disrespectful to ask since it would be so laughably easy for them. Wolf packs regularly bring down prey ranging from rabbits and white-tail deer all the way to elk, bison, and, rarely, moose. Just one wolf could overpower an adult man and deliver a critical bite with very little resistance. Against a whole pack? Yeah, say goodbye. Wolves use their numbers and angles to cut off the weakest/youngest members of a herd and then proceed to run them down into exhaustion at speeds of up to thirty-five miles per hour. Once their prey looks fatigued, they'll use those bone-cracking jaws to clamp on the panicking animal's snout and flank to bring it down. And at that point, it's credits for whatever they were chasing. In fact, the wolves' hunting ability is what originally drew us to them (or them to us, depending on how you look at it).

So yes, a wolf would have no problem putting your autobiography in the history section. But you're much more likely to get series finaled by a jaywalking deer or an electrical wire–chewing squirrel than you are to be attacked by a wolf. Hell, you have a better chance of getting turned into a statistic by the wolf's domesticated cousin than by the "big bad" himself.

In my admittedly biased opinion, few animals have been as unfairly persecuted as the wolf. They deserve better, and you can put my will on that hill because I will die on it.

WOLVERINES

FOUND IN: NORTHERN CANADA, ALASKA, NORDIC EUROPE, RUSSIA, SIBERIA
MERK RATING: 5

Someone asked me which is the Chuck Norris of animals, and the answer is simple: A wolverine. Even though they're only about fifty pounds, they've been known to take down much larger animals, like moose. (To be fair, the moose was probably already injured, but c'mon, it's still a freaking moose.) One actually merked a polar bear in the zoo by clamping his jaws around its throat and holding on until the bear suffocated. That's a dog-sized weasel putting the largest land predator on the planet in a newspaper headline.

Wolverines don't even normally hunt; they'd rather steal. Because they're scavengers, wolverines will steal from wolves, cougars, and bears and dare them to do something about it. They just don't care. And their rotating teeth can cut through bone and chew through solid frozen meat, meaning they eat every part of the animal including the teeth. They don't even have a really strong bite force. They're so stubborn that they'll keep tearing at the skin and flesh of a larger animal until it eventually passes out from shock. It's like getting shanked to death with a butter knife.

They also have a bad habit of spraying the stuff they steal with a nasty-smelling yellow liquid to make sure whoever it belongs to doesn't want it back. They'll break into cabins, stink bomb the whole place, and then walk away with something that means nothing to them but is an inconvenience to you.

Male wolverines also have multiple baby mamas in their territory that they'll visit when they feel like it, like a little pimp weasel.

" A wolverine is

A WALKING MIDDLE FINGER WITH CLAWS. "

ZEBRA

FOUND IN: AFRICA
MERK RATING: 8.5

Zebras are straight-up morally bankrupt prison stripe ponies. To be
fair, you would be too if you lived in a place where everything with a
heartbeat was considered an opp. Zebras are actually more related to
donkeys than to horses. We've never ridden them because they would
literally kick the life points out of any Dolittle that tried. First of all, they
have a boot that can crack a lion's skull and send its jaw to another
area code. Matter of fact, Google "what animal has the strongest kick"
and you'll find out that a zebra can hit you with 3,000 pounds of
force. And if you try getting friendly with this striped donkey, it will
bite the positivity right out of you.

Long story short, piss off a zebra and you'll go from seeing black and white to seeing white and then black. And the next time you see this Oreo horse getting clapped by a lion, just know this homicidal bar code probably had it coming.

And while you're at it, Google "what animal causes the most zookeeper injuries?" Yeah, zebras put more people on worker's comp than any other animal. A zookeeper at the National Zoo learned this the savage way, when a 900-pound Grevy's zebra attacked and mauled him. Not only was the zookeeper sent to the ER, the attack managed to traumatize a gazelle so badly that it ran into a barrier and snapped its own spine, killing itself.

Don't let Chris Rock distract you from the fact that Marty will commit infanticide if he has the chance. If a male sees a pregnant female, he'll literally violate her until he either forces her to miscarry or her body reabsorbs the fetus. Now if she already has a baby, the striped abortion clinic with legs will personally erase it; his favorite method is by drowning it. And he'll do it while the mother desperately tries to save her child. I'm telling you, these tiger horses are fifty shades of fucked up.

HUMANS

FOUND IN: EVERYWHERE
MERK RATING: 99

I've saved the most dangerous for last. There are a lot of deadly animals on this list, and somehow humans are by far the most destructive species to ever walk the Earth. Animals that have been around for hundreds of millions of years have been brought to their metaphorical knees by the oppressive hand of man.

You think I'm exaggerating? Sharks have been universally feared ever since *Jaws*, yet we're the ones responsible for killing about 100 million sharks a year, compared to the five to eight human lives taken by sharks. For nearly a century, wolves were hated and hunted until they were nearly extinct in forty-eight states. In comparison, you could probably count on one hand how many wild wolves have directly turned a human into past tense.

But humans aren't just a threat to wildlife everywhere. One of the most dangerous things to a human is . . . another human. If we ranked animals by their human murder count, humans themselves would nearly top the list. Hippos are known for being the most homicidal animals on the planet, and they kill an estimated 500 a year. On

average, 400,000 people are killed by humans each year. That's more than lions, tigers, bears, elephants, crocodiles, and snakes combined. Hell, technically you'd be safer in a pool with a killer whale than in an elevator full of people. The average person walks past at least sixteen murderers in their life, while a wild orca has never taken a human's life—thousands, if not millions, of seals, but never a human.

At the end of the day, as dangerous as the animals in this book can be, they're only guilty of doing what comes naturally. Because whether it's an orca slapping a seal into orbit or hyenas eating a zebra alive, it's all about survival. A young orca calf or newborn hyena cubs will starve if their mothers don't make kills to feed them. What sets us apart from animals is that animals don't possess a sense of morality (at least not to the extent of a human) and they only act out of self-preservation. However, humans possess morality and self-awareness, and we're still fucking up the world. It's not too late to save the world's species but, if we don't change, Thanos is going to look like a haunting metaphor for humanity.

" WE ARE RESPONSIBLE FOR MORE EXTINCTIONS THAN ANY OTHER CREATURES,

with an estimated 680 species that exist only in history books thanks entirely to a bipedal hominid with a superiority complex. "

ACKNOWLEDGMENTS

I would like to thank the team at both my publisher Voracious, especially Michael Szczerban and Emma Brodie, and book packager Indelible Editions for giving me the opportunity to create this book. What started as a hobby and a by-product of quarantine-induced boredom is now a printed piece of media. The same kid that was talking about animals into an Apple headphone on a social media site called TikTok is now a published author and it is all thanks to them.

I would also like to thank my management My People Know for putting me in this position in the first place, and especially Mikayla D'Agostino, for always keeping me on track and opening up an entire world of opportunities that I was previously unaware of. She's been a great manager and an even better friend.

Many thanks to Rebecca Maines and Susan Lee for making sure my text is error-free and to Butcher Billy for my amazing portraits.

And lastly and most importantly, thanks to my mother and father, Khady Toure and Lamine Ndiaye, for always encouraging the love of wildlife and nature that was present even as a 4-year-old child. Without them, I wouldn't be here (like figuratively and I literally wouldn't exist).

CREDITS, CONTINUED

Martin Prochazkacz, 195; Matthias Kiszler, 111; McGraw, 75; Michal Ninger, 32; Mikhail Gnatkovskiy, 14; Mikhail Kolesnikov, 165; Milan Zygmunt, 104; Mitchell Krog, 106; Morphart Creation, 93; MZPHOTO.CZ, 147; Natalia Tamkovich, 214; nechaevkon, 88, 163; New Imagination, 161; Nick Fox, 86; novama, 187; O'KHAEN, 66; Oded Ben-Raphael, 71; offitaly, 179; oil sc, 133; Ondrej Prosicky, 20, 97, 101, 126, 212; Onk-Q, 213; Parichart Tingnapun, 38; Patrick K. Campbell, 51; patrimonio designs ltd, 208; Paul Mason, 50; Paul Tessier, 156; Petishe, 33; Peter Hermes Furian, 212; Petr Salinger, 1; Petr Slezak, 168; Petrafler, 93; PhotocechCZ, 128; photoshooter2015, 167; phugunfire, 54; Piotr Velixar, 67; Piotr Wawrzyniuk, 78; popicon, 93; Protosov AN, 75; Prudtinai Sangwara, 134; Przemek Iciak, 77; PX Media, 95; Quatrox Production, 222; rajvish stock, 144; Ramil dolphin, 80; RantingKecildesign, 209; Ravi Patel Phera Jai, 155; Ray Kamensky, 18; Rejean Bedard, 47; reptiles4all, 34, 105, 121; Rich Carey, 188; Rich Lindie, 143; Richard Whitcombe, 223; RidiUmbrella, 35; Rini Kools, 103; Robart Mwaiteleke, 57, 107; Robert Adrian Hillman, 41; Rossillicon Photography, 175; rraya, 85; Russ Jenkins, 29; Sallye, 197; SaltedLife, 189; Sarah Magnusson, 29; SciePro, 25; Scott E Read, 122; Sergey Uryadnikov, 16, 62, 71, 114, 117, 142, 186, 196; shymar27, 216; Simon Eeman, 145; Snowboard School, 58; soratoki, 209; South O Boy, 97; SpicyTruffel, 195; Stephanie Periquet, 198; Stephen Lew, 170; Steven Giles, 153; sunwart, 40, 208; Susan Schmitz, 120; Tabata Art Studio, 58; Tanvir Ali, 148; Tanya Leanovich, 109; The Fisherman, 209; The Jungle Explorer, 51; ThiagoSantos, 103; Thorsten Spoerlein, 125; Tomas Kotouc, 186; Tony Rix, 164; Tracy Kerestesh, 23; Tristan Tan, 85; Tridsanu Thopet, 89; U. Eisenlohr, 201; Valerii_M, 128; Vectorium, 208; Vera Larina, 163; Vladimir Wrangel, 118, 192; Vladislav Klimin, 205; Vladislav T. Jirousek, 186; voy4uk, 202; Walter Mario Stein, 136; Wang LiQiang, 177; weter 777, 108; White Space Illustrations, 38; wildestanimal, 194; WildStrawberry, 69; Willyam Bradbury, 3, 70, 72; wolfness72, 218; worldclassphoto, 191; yeshaya dinerstein, 160; yod 67, 108, 114; **Tu Dong:** 212; **Wikimedia Commons:** Amada44, 205; Benjamin Freeman, 178; Jitze Couperus, 124; Siga, 179